CHICAGO PUBLIC LIBRARY

W9-BLR-458

ORIOLE PARK

OCT 12 1999

OCT 30 1999

MAR 08 2000

FEB 28 2001

MAR 23 2001

MAY 29 2001

JUL 14 2001

SEP 4 2001

SEP 29 2001

P·O·C·K·E

# INVENTIO

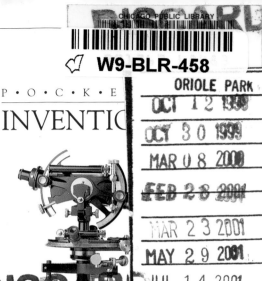

DISCARD

ORIOLE PARK BRANCH
7454 W. BALMORAL AVE.
CHICAGO, IL. 60656

FACILE BICYCLE
(1888)

FOOD MIXER
(1918)

REFLECTING TELESCOPE
(1668)

# P · O · C · K · E · T · S

# INVENTIONS

Written by
**ERYL DAVIES**

OCTANT
(c.1750)

GRAMOPHONE
(EARLY 1900S)

TECHNICOLOR
CAMERA (1932)

R01367 68483

A DK PUBLISHING BOOK

| | |
|---|---|
| **Project editor** | Mary-Clare Mitchell |
| **Art editor** | Louise Morley |
| **Senior editor** | Laura Buller |
| **Senior art editor** | Helen Senior |
| **Editorial consultant** | Susan Watt |
| **Picture research** | Giselle Harvey |
| **Production** | Louise Barratt |
| | Catherine Semark |
| **US editor** | Jill Hamilton |

First American edition, 1995
4 6 8 10 9 7 5 3

Published in the United States by
DK Publishing, Inc.,
95 Madison Avenue,
New York, New York 10016

Copyright © 1995 Dorling Kindersley Limited, London

All rights reserved under International and Pan-American Copyright
Conventions. No part of this publication may be reproduced, stored in a retrieval
system, or transmitted in any form or by any means, electronic, mechanical,
photocopying, recording, or otherwise, without the prior written permission of
the copyright owner. Published in Great Britain by Dorling Kindersley Limited.

Distributed by Houghton Mifflin Company, Boston.

Library of Congress Cataloging-in-Publication Data

Davies, Eryl, 1944–
    Inventions / by Eryl Davies. -- 1st American ed.
    p.  cm. -- (A DK pocket)
    Includes index.
    ISBN 1-56458-889-0
    1. Inventions--History--Juvenile literature. [1. Inventions--
History.] I. Title.  II. Series.
T15.D27    1995
609--dc20                                        94-24434
                                                      CIP
                                                      AC

Color reproduction by Colourscan, Singapore
Printed and bound in Italy by L.E.G.O.

# CONTENTS

CHICAGO PUBLIC LIBRARY
ORIOLE PARK BRANCH
5201 N. OKETO          60656

# HOW TO USE THIS BOOK

These pages show you how to use *Pockets: Inventions*.
The book is divided into several sections. The main
section gives detailed information about hundreds of
inventions. There is also an introductory section at
the front and a reference section at the back. Turn
to the contents or index pages for more information.

INVENTIONS
The inventions in the book have
been grouped into related subjects
and arranged into five sections –
Everyday Life, Trade and Industry,
Science and Communication, Travel
and Exploration, and Entertainment
and Leisure. An introduction page at
the beginning of each section gives
an overview of the pages that follow.

## OPTICAL INVENTIONS

MICROSCOPES, TELESCOPES, and other optical
inventions have been vital for advances in
science. Most optical devices contain lenses,
which can make small objects appear larger or
distant objects appear closer. Lenses
depend on the fact that rays
of light bend, or refract,
as they pass from
air to glass.

Corner coding

Heading

Introduction

Caption

WAY INTO THE STARS
The first telescope
was built in 1608 by
Dutchman Hans
Lippershey. It had
two lenses that
refracted the light
and made distant
objects look much
closer. A year
later, Italian
Galileo Galilei
used a similar
telescope to study
the Moon.

Telescope swivels on wooden ball

NEWTON'S REFLECTOR (1668)

MAGNIFYING WITH MIRRORS
In 1668, Isaac Newton built
the first reflecting telescope,
which used curved mirrors
instead of lenses to magnify
distant objects. It produced
much clearer images
than could be obtained
with a refracting telescope
of the time.

Label

---

CORNER CODING
Corners of the main
section pages are
color coded to
remind you which
section you are in.

EVERYDAY LIFE

TRADE AND
INDUSTRY

SCIENCE AND
COMMUNICATION

TRAVEL AND
EXPLORATION

ENTERTAINMENT
AND LEISURE

HEADING
This describes the
subject of the page.
This page is about
optical inventions.
If a subject continues
over several pages, the
heading applies.

INTRODUCTION
...vides a clear,
general overview of the
subject. After reading the
introduction, you should
have an idea of what the
following pages are about.

LABELS
To give extra clarity, some
pictures have labels. These
give extra information, or
identify a picture when it is
not obvious from the text
what it is.

## FACT BOXES

Many pages in the introductory and main sections have fact boxes. These contain at-a-glance information and provide extra facts about the subject. This fact box gives more details about optical inventions and discoveries.

## RUNNING HEADS

These remind you which section you are in. The top of the left-hand page gives the section name. The right-hand page gives the subject. This page on optical inventions is in the Science and Communication section.

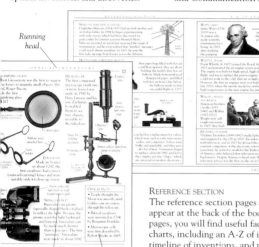

*Running head*

*Annotation*

*Fact box*

## REFERENCE SECTION

The reference section pages are yellow and appear at the back of the book. On these pages, you will find useful facts, dates, and charts, including an A-Z of inventors, a timeline of inventions, and maps of great inventing civili .

## CAPTIONS AND ANNOTATIONS

Each illustration has a caption and most have annotations. Annotations, in *italics*, point out features of an illustration and usually have leader lines.

## INDEX

There are two at the back of the book – a subject index and an index of inventors. The subject index lists each subject covered in the book. The index of inventors lists the inventors that are featured.

# INTRODUCTION TO INVENTIONS

# WHAT IS AN INVENTION?

AN INVENTION IS THE CREATION of something that didn't exist before. It can be a simple gadget, a novel process, a new material, or a complex machine. Some inventions result from the desire to fulfill specific needs; others arise by accident or evolve gradually. The bicycle, for example, is not a single invention but a combination of many individual inventions.

*Saddle*

*Adjustable seat post*

*Welded joints*

*Brakes were first used in the 1860s.*

THE BICYCLE
Many inventions, from one of the earliest (the wheel) to one of the most recent (the composite frame) can be found in a modern bicycle.

MODERN HYBRID BICYCLE

*Taut wire spokes were added to bicycle wheels in 1870.*

Gears

WHEELS
Originally made of either wood or stone, wheels were invented by the Mesopotamians more than 5,000 years ago.

*Chains were first used in 1869.*

*The gear mechanism was patented in 1896.*

## CHAINS AND GEARS

The addition of chains and gears made bicycles much easier to ride. The chain allows the pedals to be positioned under the seat rather than on the front wheel; gears enable the cyclist to ride at different speeds while pedaling normally.

*Changing gear moves the chain from one cog to another.*

### PATENT FACTS

• Inventors often apply for patents to protect their ideas.

• Patents are legal documents that stop anyone from copying or using inventors' ideas.

• The word *patent* comes from the Latin *litterae patente*, meaning "open letters."

*Handlebar*

*Brake cables were devised by Ernest Bowden in 1896.*

innondale

*Strong, lightweight frame*

## NEW MATERIALS

The earliest bicycle frames were made from wood and iron and were very cumbersome. Lighter steel frames were introduced in the 1890s, while tough composite materials appeared much more recently.

*Quick-release lever*

*Tread enables tire to grip the road.*

*Pneumatic (air-filled) tires were invented in 1888.*

*Pedals appeared in 1839.*

*Valve for filling tire with air*

# WHY DO PEOPLE INVENT?

PEOPLE INVENT FOR ALL KINDS of reasons. Some invent in order to meet basic human needs, while others invent to fulfill their own creative desires. Many inventions are inspired by social or economic reasons; by the desire to make life easier and more comfortable – or by the need to make money.

## Meeting economic demands

Making money can be a powerful incentive for invention, allowing individuals, companies, or nations to stay ahead of the competition. During the early years of textile manufacture, for example, a succession of inventions kept the wheels of industry turning.

FLYING SHUTTLE

*Shuttle holding thread*

*Device for throwing shuttle from right to left across loom*

FLYING SHUTTLE
Weaving became much faster after Englishman John Kay invented the flying shuttle in 1733. The shuttle was thrown across the loom at high speed, taking the thread with it.

HANDLOOM WITH FLYING SHUTTLE

*Drive wheel*

SPINNING FRAME
The invention of the flying shuttle meant that yarn was used up much more quickly than it c___ ___ spun. To solve this problem, variou___ ___s devised power-driven spinning machi___ ___ch machine was this spinning frame, ___ ___ard Arkwright in 1769.

ARKWRIGHT'S SPINNING FRAME (1769)

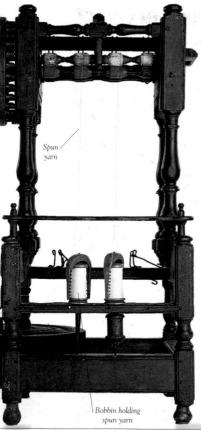

Spun yarn

Bobbin holding spun yarn

### STEAM POWER
Powered spinning then led to a surplus of yarn that could not be woven quickly enough. The balance was restored in 1787, when Edmund Cartwright built the first steam-powered loom.

COTTON GIN
(1792)

Raw cotton from which seeds are removed

### COTTON GIN
Meanwhile, in the US, the demand for raw cotton was growing. In 1792, Eli Whitney invented the cotton gin, which separate cotton from its seeds a high peed. As a result, cot luction increased dram

# Meeting social needs

For thousands of years, inventions have been inspired by the basic human needs of comfort, security, hygiene, and health. More recently, devices that make life easier or more luxurious have become increasingly popular. Whatever the reason for their creation, many inventions have had a huge impact on the way we live, and our lives would be very different without them.

LOCK AND KEY
(1700s)

*Lock mechanism*

*Iron key*

*End of key operates lock mechanism.*

*Locks contain a series of levers, which are moved by the key.*

*Dowsing bulb gives off heat.*

EARLY ELECTRIC
HEATER

### SAFETY AND SECURITY
Many devices are invented for our safety and security. In 1818, Jeremiah Chubb designed a lock mechanism to prevent burglaries at a local naval dockyard. Sadly, modern society requires many of us to install similar devices in our own homes.

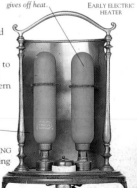

*Reflector*

### COMFORTABLE LIVING
Inventions such as heaters and air conditioning systems have been designed to make life more comfortable, either by keeping us warm in cold weather or by keeping us cool in hot weather.

## STAYING HEALTHY

By eradicating infections, or providing cures for diseases, many inventions have enabled people to live longer and healthier lives. The development of drugs and vaccines, and improvements in general hygiene, have been vital in the fight against illness.

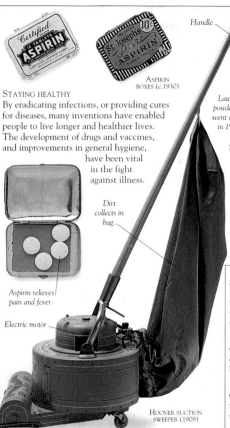

ASPIRIN BOXES (c.1930)

*Handle*

*Laundry powder first went on sale in 1907.*

*Dirt collects in bag.*

*Aspirin relieves pain and fever.*

*Electric motor*

HOOVER SUCTION SWEEPER (1908)

## SAVING TIME AND EFFORT

The desire to save time and effort around the home has inspired the invention of the vacuum cleaner, the washing machine, and many other devices. This vacuum cleaner was built by the Hoover company in 1908.

---

### INVENTION FACTS

• The first washing machines were simply wooden boxes with turning handles.

• Before the vacuum cleaner was invented, carpets had to be beaten to remove dust.

• The first vacuum cleaners were huge and needed several people to operate them.

# THE STORY OF AN INVENTION

AN INVENTION CAN take years to develop and can involve the combined efforts of many different people. The story of the sewing machine illustrates how a simple idea can evolve gradually into a complex machine, as new ideas and inventions are incorporated.

MACHINE-SEWING

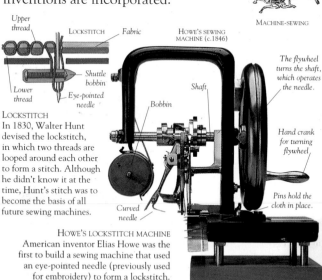

Upper thread

LOCKSTITCH    Fabric

HOWE'S SEWING MACHINE (c.1846)

Shuttle bobbin

Lower thread    Eye-pointed needle

Shaft

Bobbin

Curved needle

The flywheel turns the shaft, which operates the needle.

Hand crank for turning flywheel

Pins hold the cloth in place.

## LOCKSTITCH
In 1830, Walter Hunt devised the lockstitch, in which two threads are looped around each other to form a stitch. Although he didn't know it at the time, Hunt's stitch was to become the basis of all future sewing machines.

## HOWE'S LOCKSTITCH MACHINE
American inventor Elias Howe was the first to build a sewing machine that used an eye-pointed needle (previously used for embroidery) to form a lockstitch. Howe patented his machine in 1846.

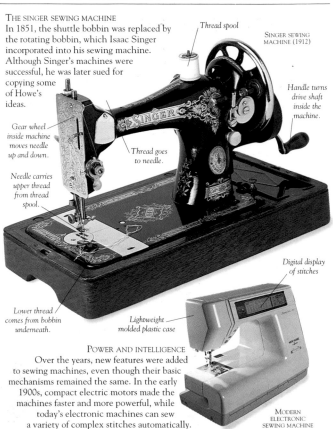

## THE SINGER SEWING MACHINE

In 1851, the shuttle bobbin was replaced by the rotating bobbin, which Isaac Singer incorporated into his sewing machine. Although Singer's machines were successful, he was later sued for copying some of Howe's ideas.

*Thread spool*

SINGER SEWING MACHINE (1912)

*Handle turns drive shaft inside the machine.*

*Gear wheel inside machine moves needle up and down.*

*Thread goes to needle.*

*Needle carries upper thread from thread spool.*

*Lower thread comes from bobbin underneath.*

*Digital display of stitches*

*Lightweight molded plastic case*

## POWER AND INTELLIGENCE

Over the years, new features were added to sewing machines, even though their basic mechanisms remained the same. In the early 1900s, compact electric motors made the machines faster and more powerful, while today's electronic machines can sew a variety of complex stitches automatically.

MODERN
ELECTRONIC
SEWING MACHINE

# FAILED INVENTIONS

INVENTIONS ARE OFTEN UNSUCCESSFUL. Some simply don't work because of a basic flaw in the inventor's understanding or knowledge. Others fail to catch on because, despite their ingenuity, they don't actually save any time or effort. Many are unreliable, expensive, or totally impractical.

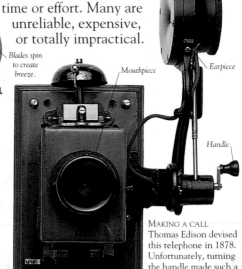

EDISON'S TELEPHONE

*Earpiece*

*Mouthpiece*

*Handle*

*Blades spin to create breeze.*

GAS-POWERED FAN

### HOT-AIR FAN
This extraordinary fan was made in 1904. Although the fan was designed to cool the air, the gas-powered motor actually gave out more heat than the fan could remove.

*Edison's telephone could be mounted on the wall.*

### MAKING A CALL
Thomas Edison devised this telephone in 1878. Unfortunately, turning the handle made such a noise that it was almost impossible to hear what the person at the other end was saying.

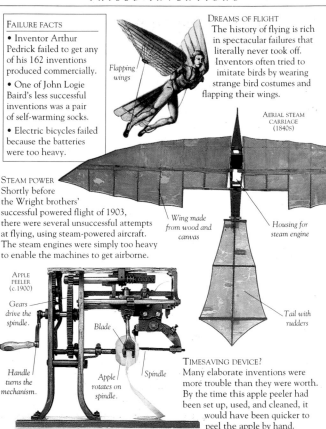

## FAILURE FACTS

- Inventor Arthur Pedrick failed to get any of his 162 inventions produced commercially.

- One of John Logie Baird's less successful inventions was a pair of self-warming socks.

- Electric bicycles failed because the batteries were too heavy.

## DREAMS OF FLIGHT

The history of flying is rich in spectacular failures that literally never took off. Inventors often tried to imitate birds by wearing strange bird costumes and flapping their wings.

*Flapping wings*

AERIAL STEAM CARRIAGE (1840s)

## STEAM POWER

Shortly before the Wright brothers' successful powered flight of 1903, there were several unsuccessful attempts at flying, using steam-powered aircraft. The steam engines were simply too heavy to enable the machines to get airborne.

*Wing made from wood and canvas*

*Housing for steam engine*

APPLE PEELER (c.1900)

*Gears drive the spindle.*

*Blade*

*Handle turns the mechanism.*

*Apple rotates on spindle.*

*Spindle*

*Tail with rudders*

## TIMESAVING DEVICE?

Many elaborate inventions were more trouble than they were worth. By the time this apple peeler had been set up, used, and cleaned, it would have been quicker to peel the apple by hand.

# EVERYDAY LIFE

# INTRODUCTION

INVENTIONS PLAY A HUGE PART in our everyday lives, either by providing us with the things we need to live comfortably and healthily, or by saving us precious time and effort as we carry out our daily tasks.

### HOME COMFORTS

The need for warmth has inspired many ingenious inventions. From wood-burning stoves to electric heaters, people have found many different ways to heat their homes. This electric heater has a series of fine wires that heat up when electricity flows through them.

ELECTRIC HEATER (1913)

*Wires give off heat.*

### TIMESAVERS

For many people, life has been made easier by the invention of clever gadgets that make light work of tedious chores. From can openers to tea makers, there are now hundreds of devices that save time around the home.

TEA MAKER (1904)

*Bell rings when tea is ready.*

*Clock*

*Tipping kettle*

*Spring*

### HEALTHY LIVING

Good sanitation and water supplies are essential for healthy living. Inventions such as the flushing toilet and sewage systems are vital for public health, especially in crowded cities.

FLUSHING TOILET (1800s)

*Wooden seat*

*China bowl*

*Water flushes in from under the rim.*

*U-bend*

JAPANESE LANTERN CLOCK

*Balance bar*

### CLOTHING

Clothes originally evolved from a need for people to protect themselves against cold or wet weather. But many modern garments, such as the brassiere, were invented to fulfill more specific needs.

BRASSIERES (1930s)

### TIMEKEEPING

Many inventions, from sundials to spring-wound watches, enable us to tell the time more accurately.

*Clarence Birdseye patented frozen food in 1929.*

### FOOD

Freezing, canning, and other preserving techniques enable foods to be kept for much longer and transported much farther.

BIRDS EYE
FROSTED FOODS
BRUSSELS SPROUTS
NET WEIGHT 10 OZ.
BIRDS EYE FOODS LTD.
PACKED FOR
UNILEVER HOUSE, LONDON E.C.4

FROZEN VEGETABLES

# HOMES AND BUILDINGS

HALF A MILLION years ago, people lived in huts that they made out of twigs and branches. By 10,000 B.C., some civilizations were using earth and stone to build more permanent homes. Since then, the invention of different materials, tools, and building techniques has made life much easier for builders, decorators, and do-it-yourself enthusiasts.

*Wedge-shaped blocks fit closely together.*

*Overlapping roof tiles help keep out the rain.*

*Mortar holds bricks together.*

## MAKING AN ENTRY

The slabs of stone used above entrances to ancient buildings were heavy and difficult to lift into position. Arches, made from smaller blocks, were easier to build. The first arches appeared in Mesopotamia about 5,000 years ago.

## BRICKS AND MORTAR

Molded bricks have been used for about 5,500 years, and the first roof tiles appeared in about 640 B.C. Mortar, a mixture of sand and cement, hardens after water has been added and is used to hold bricks together.

## STRAIGHT AND LEVEL

In 1661, Jean de Melchisedech Thevenot invented the spirit level to check that surfaces were horizontal. Modern spirit levels also allow vertical and angled surfaces to be checked.

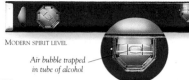

MODERN SPIRIT LEVEL

*Air bubble trapped in tube of alcohol*

## WORKMATE

In 1961, Ron Hickman devised the Workmate, a light, portable workbench. Sceptical manufacturers thought that he would be lucky to sell a few dozen, but his idea sold for a fortune.

Work surface

*The Workmate folds up and is light enough to carry.*

THE WORKMATE

## LETTING IN LIGHT

Crown glass, made by spinning bulbs of glass into sheets, was first used to make windows in 14th-century France.

EMULSION PAINT

## FINISHING TOUCHES

Water-based emulsion paints were developed in Germany in the 1930s. Emulsion paints are safer to use than oil paints because they don't give off toxic fumes and they are less likely to catch fire.

### BUILDING FACTS

• Ancient Egyptians used plumb lines to check that their pillars were vertical.

• Cement was invented in ancient Rome.

• About 500,000 million bricks are made worldwide each year.

# KEEPING WARM

FIRE WAS ONE of the most important
discoveries that humans ever made. Until
about 200 years ago, people living in cold
places were almost totally dependent on
fire for warmth. After about 1850,
gas and electricity revolutionized
heating and led to the
invention of many new
heating appliances and
systems.

*Spindle*

*Leather cord for
rotating spindle*

*Heat created
here by friction*

STARTING A FIRE
This Inuit fire stick was used about
4,000 years ago. The friction created by
rotating the spindle produced intense
heat and eventually started a fire.

*Tips covered
with chemicals*

R. BELL'S IMPROVED LUCIFERS

*Early matches
were known as
lucifers, meaning
"light bearers."*

### HEATING FACTS

• The ancient Romans
were the first to use
underfloor heating.

• Patented in 1855,
safety matches only
ignite when struck
against special surfaces.

• In 1881, Sigismund
Leoni made the first
modern gas heater.

*Wooden
splints*

THE FIRST MATCHES
Lighting fires became much easier
after the invention of matches. The first
matches were made in 1827 by British
chemist John Walker. They were tipped
with special chemicals that caught fire
when rubbed against a rough surface.

### FRANKLIN STOVE
Enclosed wood-burning stoves were improved by Benjamin Franklin in 1740. In addition to giving out more heat than open fires, they prevented sparks from flying up the chimney.

*Nichrome wire glows red-hot when electricity flows through it.*

### ELECTRIC HEATER
In 1906, American Albert Marsh invented nichrome wire, which could glow red-hot without breaking. The Belling Company used this invention to make the first radiant electric heater in 1912.

*Expansion tank keeps system full of water.*

*Copper dish reflects and intensifies the heat.*

*Radiator*

*Hot water*

*Cold water*

*Copper pipes*

*Gas boiler*

*Electric pump circulates water.*

*Wire safety grille*

ELECTRIC REFLECTOR HEATER (1930s)

### CENTRAL HEATING
Hot water has been used for heating since 1716, when Swede Marten Triewald used iron hot water pipes to heat greenhouses. Modern central heating systems, like this one, appeared after the development of compact electric pumps in the 1950s.

# Lighting

About 20,000 years ago, people discovered that they could produce light by burning oil. Oil lamps and candles were the main sources of artificial lighting until the early 19th century, when gas lights became more common. By the 1950s, most people were using electricity to light their homes.

*Wick*

SHELL LAMP

## Oil Burners

Early people burned animal fats and vegetable oils to produce light. They used hollow shells like this to hold the fuel reserves.

*Glass cover*

*Oil tank*

*Hollow wick*

*Wick adjuster*

OIL LAMP WITH HOLLOW WICK

*Wick*

## Candlelight

A candle is simply a wick surrounded by tallow or wax. As the wick burns, the tallow or wax melts and gives off light. Candles appeared in Egypt about 2,000 years ago.

*Wax*

*Snuffer extinguishes flame without giving off smoke.*

## Burning Bright

In 1784, Frenchman Aimé Argand invented an oil lamp that had a hollow, circular wick. As air rose through the center of the wick, the oil burned more efficiently and produced a much brighter flame.

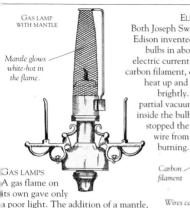

GAS LAMP
WITH MANTLE

*Mantle glows
white-hot in
the flame.*

## GAS LAMPS
A gas flame on
its own gave only
a poor light. The addition of a mantle,
a fine mesh of fibers that glows in a
flame, made the light much brighter.
The mantle was patented in 1885.

## ELECTRIC LIGHTING
Both Joseph Swan and Thomas
Edison invented electric light
bulbs in about 1880. An
electric current made the
carbon filament, or wire,
heat up and glow
brightly. A
partial vacuum
inside the bulb
stopped the
wire from
burning.

*Air is pumped
out to create
a partial
vacuum.*

*Carbon
filament*

*Wires carrying
electric current
to and from
filament*

SWAN'S
LAMP

## FLUORESCENT LIGHT
Introduced in 1935,
fluorescent light bulbs
use less electricity
than ordinary electric
bulbs. A special gas
inside the tube
produces invisible
ultraviolet light as
electricity passes
through it. This
makes the powdery
inner coating of the
tube glow brightly.

MODERN
FLUORESCENT LAMP

# MAKING LIFE EASIER

IN THE PAST, many wealthy people had servants to do their domestic chores. But as more and more people started to do these chores for themselves, devices that made household tasks easier became increasingly popular.

DOING THE LAUNDRY

## Around the home

Early household appliances relied on clever mechanisms to ease the job at hand. Many of these appliances were then improved with the addition of a compact electrical motor, which was invented by Nikola Tesla in 1899.

Drum

Motor

FISHER'S WASHING MACHINE

Handle

Bellows suck in dust and air.

Valve

COLLECTING DUST
Most early vacuum cleaners, like this one, were operated by hand. The handle worked the bellows, which sucked dust from the carpet. The first powered vacuum cleaner was built by Hubert Cecil Booth in 1901.

WASHING MACHINE
Alva Fisher's washing machine, patented in 1907, had a drum driven by an electric motor. An automatic mechanism reversed the drum's rotation from time to time so that the clothes didn't pile up.

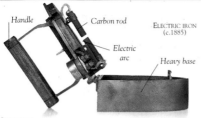

*Handle* · *Carbon rod*

ELECTRIC IRON
(c.1885)

*Electric arc*

*Heavy base*

## APPLIANCE FACTS

• Thermostats were added to electric irons in the 1930s to cope with synthetic fabrics.

• Isaac Singer initiated installment plans in order to sell his sewing machines more widely.

• During World War I, Booth used his vacuum cleaners to help rid a yellow fever hospital of germs.

IRONING

The electric iron was introduced by Henry Seely in 1882. It was heated by an electric arc – a powerful spark that jumped between the two carbon rods.

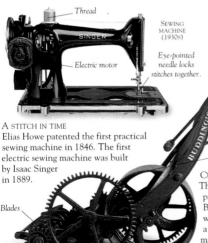

*Thread*

SEWING MACHINE
(1930s)

*Eye-pointed needle locks stitches together.*

*Electric motor*

BUDDING'S
BLADE-RUNNER
(1830)

*Lever for disconnecting the gears*

BUDDING'S PATENT N 315T

*Roller*

A STITCH IN TIME

Elias Howe patented the first practical sewing machine in 1846. The first electric sewing machine was built by Isaac Singer in 1889.

*Blades*

CUTTING THE GRASS

The first lawn mower was patented by Englishman Edwin Budding in 1830. The roller was connected to the blades via a series of gearwheels, which made the blades turn 12 times faster than the roller.

# In the kitchen

Labor-saving devices in the kitchen are welcomed by lazy people, busy people, and enthusiastic cooks alike. Food can now be prepared and cooked more easily than ever before. As with other inventions, electricity has played a key role in the development of many kitchen appliances.

KETTLE ON SPIRIT STOVE

*Heating element*

SWAN'S ELECTRIC KETTLE
Until the 1920s, electric kettles had external heating elements. But the "Swan" kettle of 1921 was more efficient because the heating element was actually in the water.

*Switch to control hot plates*

*Electric burner*

COOKING WITH ELECTRICITY
The first domestic electric stove was made by the Carpenter Company in the US in 1891. Gas stoves were already common, so electricity companies advertised the safety and economy of their new stoves. Even so, electric and gas stoves are now equally popular.

### POP-UP TOASTER

Charles Strite, a mechanic from Minnesota, designed the first automatic toaster in 1927. As with modern toasters, the slices of bread rested on a spring-loaded rack and were toasted by an electric heating element. Sliced bread appeared in stores a year later.

*Time control knob*

MODERN FOOD PROCESSOR

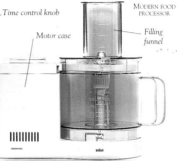

*Filling funnel*

*Motor case*

### PROCESSING FOOD

Compact electric motors led to the invention of numerous powered mixers and blenders. In 1971, Frenchman Pierre Verdon designed the modern food processor, with a high-speed chopping blade and electronic speed control.

*Teflon's nonstick properties make light work of frying eggs.*

### NONSTICK FRYING

Discovered in 1941 by American Roy Plunkett, Teflon (polymerized tetrafluoroethylene) was patented for kitchenware in 1960. It is now used as a nonstick coating on all kinds of objects, from skillets to irons.

# FOOD AND DRINK

MUCH OF WHAT we eat and drink today is
days, weeks, or even months old. People
have devised different methods for
preserving food and for ensuring
that it is safe to eat. Some of
these methods have been used
since ancient times; others
result from more recent
advances in science
and technology.

### SALTING
A good coating
of salt is one of the
oldest methods for
preserving fish. The salt
creates an environment that
discourages bacterial growth.
Before it is used, the salted fish
must be soaked in water.

SALTED
COD

*Lid keeps can
airtight.*

### CANNED FOOD
In 1810, Frenchman
Nicolas Appert devised
a way of preserving
food in sealed
containers. He heated
the food in a glass jar
and sealed the top with
cork. Peter Durand
developed this idea
and, in 1811, produced
the first canned food.

TIN CAN

### PASTEURIZATION
In 1860, Louis Pasteur found
that heating wine to 158°F
(70°C) killed the bacteria
that caused souring. This
technique is now used to
treat – or pasteurize – milk.

*Press-button tap*

WINECASK
INSERT

## WINECASK

Once a bottle of wine has been uncorked, the wine comes into contact with the air and quickly goes sour. In 1965, Australian inventor Thomas Angove solved this problem by devising the winecask, a cardboard box with a plastic insert. As wine is drawn from the cask, the plastic insert collapses and the remaining wine stays fresh.

*Freezing compartment*

## KEEPING COOL

Electric refrigerators appeared in the 1920s and revolutionized food storage. A special fluid, which vaporizes at low temperatures, is pumped through pipes in the refrigerator and keeps the contents cool.

*Insulated walls*

*Electric motor and pump*

*Coil gives out waste heat.*

KELVINATOR REFRIGERATOR
(c.1922)

## FOOD FACTS

- The can opener was not invented until 44 years after the arrival of canned food.

- American Clarence Birdseye patented fast-frozen food in 1929.

- Engineer Ermal Fraze invented the ring-pull can in 1959.

# CLOTHING

CLOTHES WERE ORIGINALLY invented to protect people against the elements. As civilizations developed, people made clothes for more specific purposes and devised ways to improve their clothes by making them warmer, more waterproof, or simply easier to get on and off.

*Braided wool fastening*

AZTEC SANDAL

FOOTWEAR
Early people devised various kinds of footwear to protect their feet from hard and stony ground. Many shoes, like this Aztec sandal, were made from plant fibers.

*Sole made from fiber of aloe plant*

ZIPPING UP
In 1893, American Whitcomb Judson invented a sliding device with interlocking teeth that he used for fastening boots. Unfortunately, his device tended to jam or burst open. In 1914, Gideon Sundback made the first zipper to be used for clothing.

*Waterproof fabric*

*Tape for attaching zipper to garment*

*Slide forces teeth together and apart.*

*Teeth lock together.*

*Handle*

IN THE RAIN
Collapsible umbrellas were in use before 1800 but were very heavy. In 1848 Samuel Fox introduced steel frames, which were much lighter.

EARLY ZIPPER

**BLUE JEANS**

Jeans were first made in 1874 by Jacob Davis and Levi Strauss. They were designed for gold miners, who complained that their ordinary trousers wore out too quickly.

*Copper rivets reinforce seams.*

*Rubber-coated fabric*

**STAYING DRY**

Thanks to Charles Macintosh, whose method of waterproofing fabric has been applied to boots as well as coats, it is possible to walk through puddles without getting wet feet.

*Strong seam*

*Jeans are made of denim, a tough cotton fabric.*

*Molded rubber sole*

**LYCRA**

Introduced in 1959, Lycra was originally intended for underwear. Its figure-hugging qualities make it ideal for all kinds of clothing, from swimwear to socks.

*Lycra is light and stretchy.*

LYCRA LEGGINGS

**CLOTHING FACTS**

• The ancient Romans developed shoes fitted for left and right feet.

• Bloomers were introduced in America in 1851 by Amelia Bloomer, the women's rights campaigner.

• Velcro was patented in 1956 by Georges de Mestral of Switzerland, who was fed up with zippers that jammed.

# HYGIENE AND HEALTH

KEEPING CLEAN NOT ONLY MAKES life more pleasant for ourselves and our companions, but also helps discourage infection and disease. Clean water and good sanitation are essential for healthy living, while drugs and medicines can both prevent and fight infections and illness.

## CLEAN WATER

In 1804, Scotsman John Gibb built a filter, like the one shown below, that was large enough to supply the whole city of Paisley in Scotland with clean water. As rainwater flowed through the layers of sand, gravel, and stones, the impurities in the water were filtered out.

## SHOWERS

The first showers are thought to date back to 1350 B.C. This Greek vase painting from about 600 B.C. shows a communal shower that appears to have nozzles for the water.

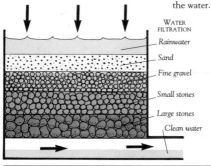

WATER FILTRATION

Rainwater

Sand

Fine gravel

Small stones

Large stones

Clean water

## SOAP

Soap is made by boiling fats with caustic soda. Cheap mass-produced soap first became available in the early 1800s, after the introduction of synthetic soda.

## HEALTH FACTS

• All drugs were given orally until 1853, when C. Pravaz invented the hypodermic syringe.

• Toilet paper was invented in 1857.

• In 1945, Fleming, Chain, and Florey were awarded the Nobel prize for medicine, for their work on penicillin.

## PREVENTING DISEASE

Vaccines help people develop immunity to diseases. The first successful vaccine, which prevented smallpox, was produced in 1796 by Edward Jenner.

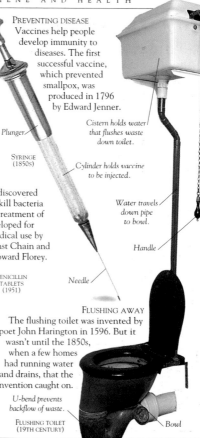

*Cistern holds water that flushes waste down toilet.*

*Plunger*

SYRINGE
(1850s)

*Cylinder holds vaccine to be injected.*

*Water travels down pipe to bowl.*

*Handle*

## FIGHTING INFECTION

In 1928, Alexander Fleming discovered penicillin, a mold that could kill bacteria and was to revolutionize the treatment of infections. The drug was developed for medical use by Ernst Chain and Howard Florey.

PENICILLIN TABLETS
(1951)

*Needle*

## FLUSHING AWAY

The flushing toilet was invented by poet John Harington in 1596. But it wasn't until the 1850s, when a few homes had running water and drains, that the invention caught on.

10 TROCHES
**PENIGUM**
(SUGAR-COATED)
PENICILLIN CHEWING TROCHES

Chewing troche contains 10,000 Units of
Procaine Penicillin G.
OC 0035230        APR.53
To be dispensed only by or on the pre...
physician or dentist.
Supplied by
NE S. E. MASSENGILL CO., Bristol, Tenn.

*U-bend prevents backflow of waste.*

FLUSHING TOILET
(19TH CENTURY)

*Bowl*

# KEEPING TIME

BEFORE PENDULUM CLOCKS were invented, people relied on the position of the sun to tell the time. They also invented hourglasses and other devices for measuring fixed periods of time. Since the 1960s, mechanical clocks and watches have been replaced by electrical and electronic devices.

SUNDIAL (1700s)

Gnomon

Dial marked off in hours

### PENDULUM CLOCK

In the 1580s, Italian Galileo Galilei suggested using the regular swing of a pendulum to control a clock. The first pendulum clock was made in 1657 by Dutch scientist Christiaan Huygens.

*Each swing of the pendulum moves the clock hands forward.*

*Weight drives clock mechanism.*

PENDULUM CLOCK

### CASTING A SHADOW

Shadow clocks, the forerunners of sundials, were used in Egypt and China about 4,000 years ago. The Arabs developed more accurate sundials with sloping gnomons – rods that cast a shadow on the dial.

Narrow hole

### RUNNING OUT OF TIME

In the 1st century A.D., the Romans used hourglasses to keep time. The sand took a fixed amount of time to flow through the hole from the top to the bottom of the glass.

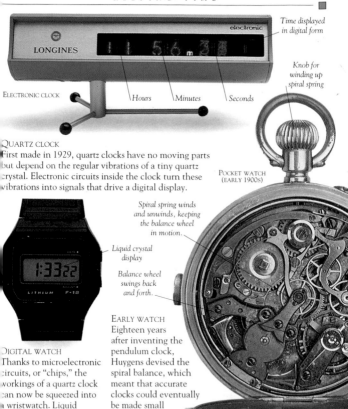

Time displayed in digital form

ELECTRONIC CLOCK

Hours

Minutes

Seconds

Knob for winding up spiral spring

## QUARTZ CLOCK

First made in 1929, quartz clocks have no moving parts but depend on the regular vibrations of a tiny quartz crystal. Electronic circuits inside the clock turn these vibrations into signals that drive a digital display.

POCKET WATCH
(EARLY 1900s)

Spiral spring winds and unwinds, keeping the balance wheel in motion.

Liquid crystal display

Balance wheel swings back and forth.

## DIGITAL WATCH

Thanks to microelectronic circuits, or "chips," the workings of a quartz clock can now be squeezed into a wristwatch. Liquid crystal displays were invented in the 1970s.

## EARLY WATCH

Eighteen years after inventing the pendulum clock, Huygens devised the spiral balance, which meant that accurate clocks could eventually be made small enough to fit into a pocket.

4 3

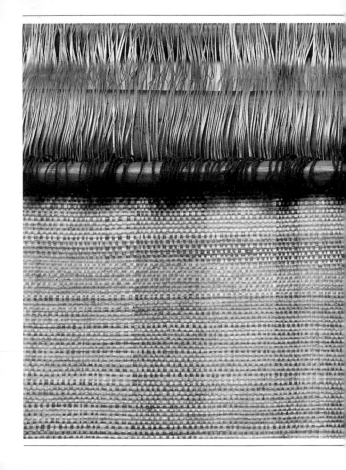

# TRADE AND
# INDUSTRY

# INTRODUCTION

INDUSTRY INVOLVES MAKING GOODS or providing services, and trade depends on the ability to buy and sell them. The invention of money, weights, and measures has played an important part in the development of trade, while the ability to both harness energy and make large-scale machinery has enabled industry to flourish.

*Wicker purse for carrying shells*

INDIAN COWRIE SHELLS

*Cowrie shells*

*Arm with scale*

*Steelyards were easy to carry and were popular with traveling merchants.*

STEELYARD (17TH CENTURY)

*Movable weight*

*Hooks on which goods are hung*

## MAKING PAYMENTS

Money began as tokens that were exchanged for goods and services. In some prehistoric societies, cowrie shells like these were used as money. Coins and banknotes were invented later.

## WEIGHING AND MEASURING

It would be impossible for people to trade without knowing the quantity of the goods changing hands. To prevent arguments about this, people devised various methods of measuring length, volume, and weight.

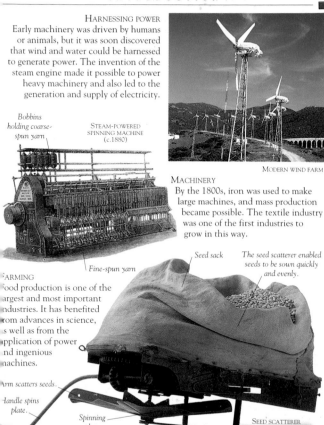

## HARNESSING POWER

Early machinery was driven by humans or animals, but it was soon discovered that wind and water could be harnessed to generate power. The invention of the steam engine made it possible to power heavy machinery and also led to the generation and supply of electricity.

*Bobbins holding coarse-spun yarn*

STEAM-POWERED SPINNING MACHINE (c.1880)

MODERN WIND FARM

## MACHINERY

By the 1800s, iron was used to make large machines, and mass production became possible. The textile industry was one of the first industries to grow in this way.

*Fine-spun yarn*

*Seed sack*

*The seed scatterer enabled seeds to be sown quickly and evenly.*

## FARMING

Food production is one of the largest and most important industries. It has benefited from advances in science, as well as from the application of power and ingenious machines.

*Arm scatters seeds.*

*Handle spins plate.*

*Spinning plate*

SEED SCATTERER (19TH CENTURY)

# BUYING AND SELLING

BEFORE THE INVENTION of money, people used to trade by barter. In other words, they simply exchanged one item or service for another. Gradually, people began to use tokens, then coins and banknotes to pay for goods. Today, money transactions are often made by computer and do not involve any cash at all.

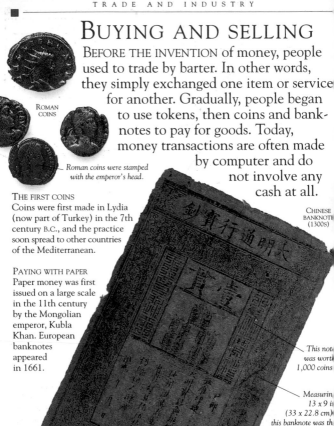

ROMAN COINS

*Roman coins were stamped with the emperor's head.*

THE FIRST COINS
Coins were first made in Lydia (now part of Turkey) in the 7th century B.C., and the practice soon spread to other countries of the Mediterranean.

PAYING WITH PAPER
Paper money was first issued on a large scale in the 11th century by the Mongolian emperor, Kubla Khan. European banknotes appeared in 1661.

CHINESE BANKNOTE (1300S)

*This note was worth 1,000 coins.*

*Measuring 13 x 9 in (33 x 22.8 cm) this banknote was the largest ever issued.*

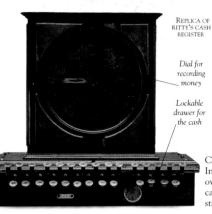

REPLICA OF
RITTY'S CASH
REGISTER

Dial for
recording
money

Lockable
drawer for
the cash

## MONEY FACTS

• Milled edging was invented to stop people from filing pieces of metal from coin edges.

• The world's first cash dispensing machine was installed in London in 1967.

• There are about 600 million credit cards in circulation worldwide.

CASH REGISTER
In 1879, American saloon-bar owner James Ritty invented the cash register to stop dishonest staff from stealing cash.

PAYING BY CHECK
Checks are simply signed instructions to banks to pay money directly from one account to another. The first check was handled by British bankers Clayton and Morris in 1659.

Bank account
number

Check must be
signed here.

MODERN CHECK

BARCLAYS
HIGH STREET, CAXTON, LONDON, N99 4XX

Pay

SPECIMEN

£

A N OTHER

BARCLAYCARD  MasterCard

5301 2500 0123

PLASTIC MONEY
Credit cards enable people to buy goods or services and pay for them later with cash or a check. The first credit card was issued in 1950 by the Diner's Club and could be used in any one of 27 restaurants in New York.

# WEIGHTS AND MEASURES

SINCE TRADING BEGAN, people have invented different ways of weighing and measuring goods. Initially, people simply used their hands or arms to compare things, but advances in trade demanded more accurate methods. The first systems of weights and measures were devised in ancient times by the Egyptians and the Babylonians.

GOLD WEIGHTS
(1700S)

**STANDARD WEIGHTS**
These decorative gold weights were made and used by the Ashanti people, who rose to power in Africa during the 18th century.

*Horizontal arm with scale*

ROMAN STEELYARD

*Pivot*

*Weight is moved along arm.*

*Scale pan holds goods to be weighed.*

---

**MEASUREMENT FACTS**

• An inch was initially measured as the width of the thumb.

• The metric system of measurement was introduced in France in 1795.

• The foot is derived from the Romans, who used a soldier's foot as a unit of length.

---

**BALANCING ACT**
Steelyards like this were invented by the Romans and used for weighing out food and crops. The weight was moved along the arm until it balanced with the scale pan. The measurement was then read from the scale.

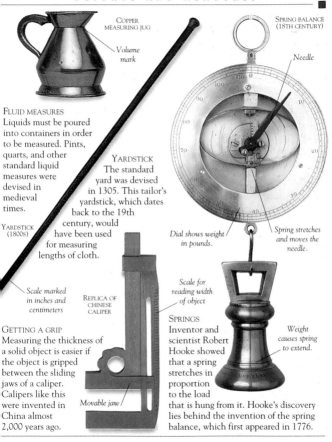

COPPER
MEASURING JUG

*Volume mark*

SPRING BALANCE
(18TH CENTURY)

*Needle*

FLUID MEASURES
Liquids must be poured
into containers in order
to be measured. Pints,
quarts, and other
standard liquid
measures were
devised in
medieval
times.

YARDSTICK
The standard
yard was devised
in 1305. This tailor's
yardstick, which dates
back to the 19th
century, would
have been used
for measuring
lengths of cloth.

YARDSTICK
(1800S)

*Scale marked
in inches and
centimeters*

REPLICA OF
CHINESE
CALIPER

*Dial shows weight
in pounds.*

*Spring stretches
and moves the
needle.*

*Scale for
reading width
of object*

GETTING A GRIP
Measuring the thickness of
a solid object is easier if
the object is gripped
between the sliding
jaws of a caliper.
Calipers like this
were invented in
China almost
2,000 years ago.

*Movable jaw*

SPRINGS
Inventor and
scientist Robert
Hooke showed
that a spring
stretches in
proportion
to the load

*Weight
causes spring
to extend.*

that is hung from it. Hooke's discovery
lies behind the invention of the spring
balance, which first appeared in 1776.

# INDUSTRIAL INVENTIONS

LARGE-SCALE INDUSTRY involves using power and machinery to manufacture goods. Inventions have led to huge changes in industry by providing new sources of power, materials, and manufacturing techniques.

## Energy and power

One of the keys to industrial growth was the ability to harness energy. Before the 1700s, most factories depended on wind or water for power. But industry was transformed by the arrival of the steam engine, which could provide power for large factories and mines.

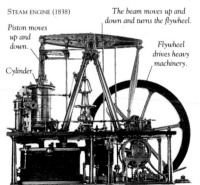

STEAM ENGINE (1838)

*The beam moves up and down and turns the flywheel.*

Piston moves up and down.

*Flywheel drives heavy machinery.*

Cylinder

WATERWHEEL
By 70 B.C., the Romans were using waterwheels to grind grain and press olives. Water power was later used to drive heavy machinery in cotton mills and other factories.

THE STEAM ENGINE
Thomas Newcomen invented the steam engine in 1712. Early steam engines were simply used for pumping, but later engines could turn wheels and heavy machinery as well.

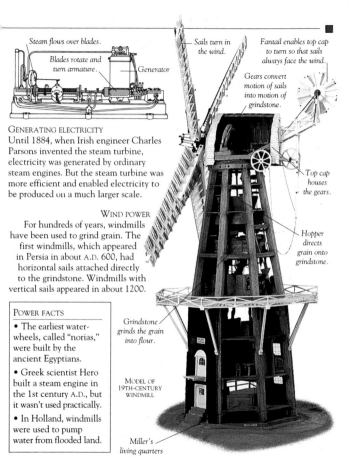

Steam flows over blades.

Blades rotate and turn armature.

Generator

Sails turn in the wind.

Fantail enables top cap to turn so that sails always face the wind.

Gears convert motion of sails into motion of grindstone.

Top cap houses the gears.

## GENERATING ELECTRICITY

Until 1884, when Irish engineer Charles Parsons invented the steam turbine, electricity was generated by ordinary steam engines. But the steam turbine was more efficient and enabled electricity to be produced on a much larger scale.

Hopper directs grain onto grindstone.

## WIND POWER

For hundreds of years, windmills have been used to grind grain. The first windmills, which appeared in Persia in about A.D. 600, had horizontal sails attached directly to the grindstone. Windmills with vertical sails appeared in about 1200.

Grindstone grinds the grain into flour.

### POWER FACTS

• The earliest water-wheels, called "norias," were built by the ancient Egyptians.

• Greek scientist Hero built a steam engine in the 1st century A.D., but it wasn't used practically.

• In Holland, windmills were used to pump water from flooded land.

MODEL OF 19TH-CENTURY WINDMILL

Miller's living quarters

# Spinning and weaving

WOVEN
FABRIC

People started to make cloth about 10,000 years ago, using simple machines to spin and weave the yarn. The arrival of spinning wheels and looms meant that cloth could be made much more quickly, but it wasn't until the 1800s, when spinning and weaving became fully mechanized, that the textile industry began to flourish.

SPINNING WHEEL
Fibers were originally twisted into thread on simple spindles, but the spinning wheel speeded up the process. The wheel was turned with the right hand, while the wool to be spun was held in the left.

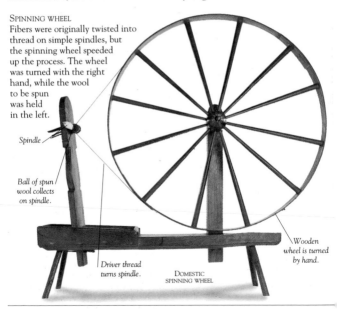

*Spindle*

*Ball of spun wool collects on spindle.*

*Driver thread turns spindle.*

DOMESTIC
SPINNING WHEEL

*Wooden wheel is turned by hand.*

JACQUARD LOOM
(EARLY 1800s)

*Punched cards program the loom to weave patterns.*

## THE COTTON GIN
Before cotton can be spun, the fiber must be removed from the seeds. This used to be a tedious task, but in 1792 American Eli Whitney invented the cotton gin, which did the job in a fraction of the time.

*Raw cotton*

## PATTERNED FABRICS
Weaving patterns was hard until 1805, when Joseph-Marie Jacquard devised a programmable loom. The loom was controlled by punched cards, on which the designs were stored.

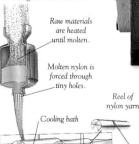

*Raw materials are heated until molten.*

*Molten nylon is forced through tiny holes.*

*Cooling bath*

*Reel of nylon yarn*

*Seedless cotton collects here.*

MODEL OF COTTON GIN
(1792)

## NYLON SPINNING
Nylon plastic was first spun into yarn in the late 1930s. The process involves forcing molten nylon through tiny holes so that it solidifies into slender fibers. The fibers are then spun into a single thread and wound onto a reel.

# Metalworking

Metals are so important that two periods in history, the Bronze Age and the Iron Age, have been named after them. The large-scale production of iron made it possible to build heavy machinery and was vital for industrial development.

ALUMINUM FOIL FOOD WRAP

WORKING WITH BRONZE
Bronze is a mixture of tin and copper and was first made in about 3500 B.C. It was melted down and cast into different shapes. Once set, it was strong and did not corrode, so it was ideal for making swords and daggers.

ALUMINUM
Aluminum, the most common metal on Earth, was discovered in 1825 by Danish scientist Hans Oersted. Light and easily shaped, it is made into all kinds of things, from food wrap to airplanes.

ROMAN IRON NAILS (A.D. 88)

*Edges could be reshapened.*

*Early iron objects were hammered into shape.*

BRONZE SWORD

HARD AS NAILS
When it is heated, iron softens enough to be hammered into shape. From 1500 B.C., iron was used in this way to make nails and other objects.

## METAL FACTS

• The Greeks and Romans made mirrors from polished bronze.

• In prehistoric times, people extracted iron from meteors that fell from the sky.

• Mercury is liquid at room temperature and is used in thermometers and tooth fillings.

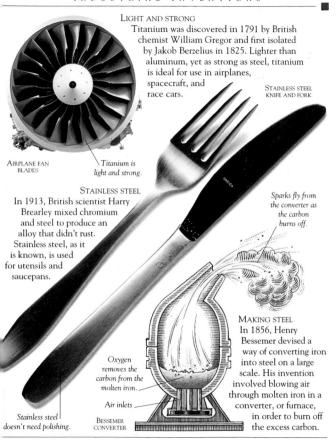

### LIGHT AND STRONG

Titanium was discovered in 1791 by British chemist William Gregor and first isolated by Jakob Berzelius in 1825. Lighter than aluminum, yet as strong as steel, titanium is ideal for use in airplanes, spacecraft, and race cars.

AIRPLANE FAN BLADES

*Titanium is light and strong.*

STAINLESS STEEL KNIFE AND FORK

### STAINLESS STEEL

In 1913, British scientist Harry Brearley mixed chromium and steel to produce an alloy that didn't rust. Stainless steel, as it is known, is used for utensils and saucepans.

*Sparks fly from the converter as the carbon burns off.*

### MAKING STEEL

In 1856, Henry Bessemer devised a way of converting iron into steel on a large scale. His invention involved blowing air through molten iron in a converter, or furnace, in order to burn off the excess carbon.

*Oxygen removes the carbon from the molten iron.*

*Air inlets*

BESSEMER CONVERTER

*Stainless steel doesn't need polishing.*

# Synthetic materials

Plastics and other synthetic materials are made by chemically combining simpler substances into polymers (long chains of atoms). Plastics are strong and easily molded and were originally used for making decorative items and toys. Nowadays they are important engineering materials as well.

BAKELITE PITCHER

Heat-resistant plastic

SMOOTH AS SILK

In 1934, American Wallace Hume Carothers and his team produced nylon, a silklike plastic that could be woven into cloth. Nylon stockings went on sale five years later and were an instant sensation.

THE FIRST PLASTIC

In 1909, Belgian chemist Leo Baekeland made the first truly synthetic plastic. Bakelite, as it was known, was made from substances found in coal tar. It did not conduct electricity or heat and was used to make all kinds of things, from pitchers to radio sets.

Nylon is sheer and hard-wearing.

Carbon-fiber frames are stronger and lighter than wooden ones.

Nylon stockings were first made in 1939.

Synthetic strings

NYLON STOCKINGS

CARBON-FIBER TENNIS RACKET

### SYNTHETIC RUBBER

The first synthetic rubber gloves, made in 1952, were intended for surgical and industrial use. Household rubber gloves were launched by the London Rubber Company in 1961.

CELLULOID PURSE (1900)

Clasp

Braided leather strap

Leather tassle

Molded celluloid resembles intricately carved ivory.

Raised pattern increases grip.

HOUSEHOLD RUBBER GLOVES

### IVORY SUBSTITUTE

Celluloid is a semisynthetic plastic made from cellulose, a plant fiber. First produced in 1869 by John Wesley Hyatt, celluloid was used to make film rolls for cameras as well as imitation ivory items like this evening purse.

### POLYETHYLENE

Discovered accidentally by British scientist R. Gibson in 1933, polyethylene is a tough, waterproof plastic, ideal for making food containers.

FOOD CONTAINERS

### COMPOSITES

Plastics can be combined with carbon fibers to make composite materials that are light and strong.

Handle

# Mass production

When goods are manufactured in large quantities, they are cheaper to produce and more people can afford to buy them. The invention of the assembly line, interchangeable part manufacture, and other timesaving devices have all helped to make mass production possible.

MODEL T
FORD (1913)

DRILL BIT
In 1865, F.W. Taylor devised a special form of steel that could withstand heavy use. Drill bits made from this steel could be used again and again without getting blunt.

Mass-produced
Model Ts were
available only
in black.

Sidelight

Radiator

Horn

Headlight

Starting
handle

Wooden-
spoked wheel

ASSEMBLY LINE
The Model T Ford was the first car to be built on a moving assembly line. Cars moved along a conveyer, and each worker fitted just one part, cutting the time taken to build a car from 12 hours to less than 2 hours.

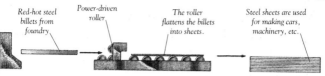

Red-hot steel billets from foundry

Power-driven roller

The roller flattens the billets into sheets.

Steel sheets are used for making cars, machinery, etc.

## ROLLING MILL
First built in 1926, large-scale rolling mills were vital for the growth of modern industry. Rolling mills supply factories with steel rolled into sheets, rods, or bars of uniform thickness and quality.

## WELDING
In 1890, Russian Nikolai Slavyanov invented electric arc welding, a quick and easy way of joining metals. An electric current creates a spot of heat on the metal so that the two pieces of metal fuse.

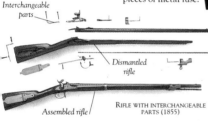

Interchangeable parts

Dismantled rifle

Assembled rifle

RIFLE WITH INTERCHANGEABLE PARTS (1855)

## INTERCHANGEABLE PARTS
Developed in the 1800s, interchangeable parts were used widely in the manufacture of rifles. The parts could be fitted easily into any rifle, saving precious minutes on the assembly line.

## UNTOUCHED BY HUMAN HANDS
Since the 1970s, robots have been used to replace human workers on production lines. The first robots could only move things from one place to another, but robots can now reproduce a range of human movements; and without getting tired.

# ARTS AND CRAFTS

MANY OF TODAY'S CRAFTS originated hundreds, or even thousands, of years ago and depend on simple inventions that were revolutionary in their time. These crafts have been kept alive because many people still value handmade products in an age when most things are made by machine.

POTTER'S WHEEL

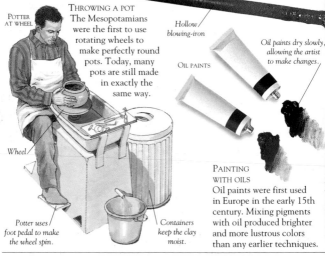

POTTER AT WHEEL

### THROWING A POT

The Mesopotamians were the first to use rotating wheels to make perfectly round pots. Today, many pots are still made in exactly the same way.

*Hollow blowing-iron*

*Oil paints dry slowly, allowing the artist to make changes.*

OIL PAINTS

*Wheel*

*Potter uses foot pedal to make the wheel spin.*

*Containers keep the clay moist.*

### PAINTING
WITH OILS

Oil paints were first used in Europe in the early 15th century. Mixing pigments with oil produced brighter and more lustrous colors than any earlier techniques.

*Knitting needles*

*Wool*

*Lace*

*Bobbin*

*Thread*

KNITTING

The earliest evidence of knitting is the remains of an Arabian sock that dates back to 700 B.C. Despite the invention of knitting machines, hand-knitting is still a popular pastime.

*Glass is blown into a bulb shape.*

*Beads weigh bobbin down to keep thread straight.*

LACEMAKING

The art of lacemaking originated in France and Belgium during the 14th century. Long needles, or bobbins, are braided over and under each other to create patterns in the lace.

*Molten glass falls into mold.*

*Mold is used to measure out correct quantity of glass.*

*Strong shears*

GLASSBLOWING

In about 100 B.C., Syrian glassworkers found that a blob of molten glass on the end of a pipe could be blown into a bulb. This technique was used to make goblets and other items and is still used today to make handblown glassware.

# FARMING

BEFORE THE GROWTH OF INDUSTRY, most people worked on the land and produced their own food. But as people moved to the cities to work, they began to rely on the remaining farmers to supply them with food. Inventions that enabled farmers to produce more crops with less labor became widely used.

PREHISTORIC FARMING TOOLS

## Cultivating the land

The development of pest control and artificial fertilizers meant that crops could be grown more abundantly. Labor-saving devices were then needed to ease the tasks of working the soil and harvesting. With the arrival of iron and steel, and the invention of the internal combustion engine, farming soon became mechanized.

*Handle is turned to lift water.*

*Water*

*Water moves up tube.*

LIFTING WATER
In about 236 B.C., Greek inventor Archimedes gave his name to a screw pump, which used the principle of the inclined plane to lift water. The pump was later used for raising water from low-lying rivers and canals in order to water crops on higher land.

*End of plow was attached to a team of horses or oxen.*

WOODEN PLOW (1763)

*Coulter slices a furrow in the ground.*

### COMBINE HARVESTER

In 1838, Americans J. Hascall and Hiram Moore built a machine that could cut the crop and put the grain into sacks. Their machine was so large that it needed more than 30 mules to pull it. The first self-propelled combine appeared in 1910.

*Threshing cylinder separates the grain from the heads.*

*Auger unloads the grain.*

*Cutter slices crop stalks.*

*Conveyor carries stalks to threshing cylinder.*

MODERN COMBINE HARVESTER

### CROP-DUSTING

Applying fertilizers and pesticides to huge fields can be very time consuming, so it makes sense to spray them from low-flying airplanes. This was first done in the US in 1925.

*Handles allow farmer to control the depth and direction of the cut.*

*Stalks tied into sheaves here.*

MODEL OF McCORMICK'S REAPER

*Horse was attached here.*

*Moldboard lifts and turns the soil.*

### THE PLOW

The plow was one of the most important innovations in agriculture. It appeared in Mesopotamia in 3500 B.C. The addition of wheels in the 10th century made the plow easier to control.

*Cutter bar*

### REAPING MACHINE

In 1834, American Cyrus McCormick devised a horse-drawn reaping machine that could both cut the grain and tie it into sheaves. In 1851, McCormick's invention won him a medal at the Great Exhibition in London.

# Animal farming and fishing

Rearing animals and catching fish demand a great deal of time and effort. From the automatic milking machine to the power-driven sheep shearer, time-saving gadgets and machinery or inventions that make farming easier have been vital for making both animal farming and fishing more profitable.

HYDRAULIC COW MILKER (1868)

MILKING MACHINE
Powered milking machines appeared in the 1880s but, like earlier hand-operated machines, they were painful for the cows. In 1895, Scotsman Alexander Shields made a gentler machine that used a pulsating vacuum to mimic a suckling calf.

SHEARING SHEEP
One of the first sets of power-driven wool clippers was made by Frederick Wolseley in 1868. Wolseley later became famous as a car maker, with his partner Herbert Austin.

BARBED WIRE
The use of barbed wire to fence off areas of land made cattle farming much less labor intensive and put many cowboys out of work. Barbed wire was patented by American farmer Joseph Glidden in 1874.

*Sharp barbs keep animals inside fenced-off land.*

BARBED WIRE (1800s)

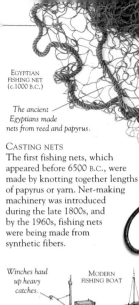

EGYPTIAN FISHING NET
(c.1000 B.C.)

*The ancient Egyptians made nets from reed and papyrus.*

## CASTING NETS

The first fishing nets, which appeared before 6500 B.C., were made by knotting together lengths of papyrus or yarn. Net-making machinery was introduced during the late 1800s, and by the 1960s, fishing nets were being made from synthetic fibers.

## FISHHOOKS

The discovery of copper and bronze meant that metal fishhooks could be made and used for fishing on a smaller scale than with nets. The cunning addition of the barb, which trapped the fish once it had bitten, appeared in about 3000 B.C.

*Hook attaches to fishing line.*

EARLY FISHHOOKS

*Barbed end*

*Winches haul up heavy catches.*

MODERN FISHING BOAT

*Fish are trapped in the net.*

## TRAWLING FOR FISH

Large-scale fishing took off in the 1880s, when steam engines were fitted to fishing boats. The boats dragged nets through the water behind them, sweeping up larger catches than ever before.

# SCIENCE AND COMMUNICATION

# INTRODUCTION

INVENTION AND SCIENTIFIC DISCOVERY often go hand in hand. Discoveries can lead to important inventions, while inventions can give scientists the means to both confirm their theories and make new discoveries.

ELECTRONIC
CALCULATOR

*Keypad*

### BEYOND VISION

Optical inventions such as microscopes and telescopes led to advances in astronomy and biology, allowing scientists to see things that they had never seen before, from distant galaxies to tiny microorganisms.

MICROSCOPE
(1728)

### ADDING UP

Many devices, from abacuses to electronic calculators, have been invented to help with counting and computing.

### UNDERSTANDING THE WEATHER

Barometers, thermometers, and other weather-measuring instruments have enabled scientists to learn more about the climate and to predict weather patterns.

*Lens focuses light.*

*Stage holds specimen.*

*Tilting mirror*

*Pointer indicates air pressure.*

ANEROID
BAROMETER

MEDICINE AND SURGERY
Advances in biology and
chemistry have helped
scientists gain a better
understanding of the
human body and its
diseases. Developments in
technology have helped them
to diagnose and treat those diseases.

Pelvic
socket

MODERN
ARTIFICIAL
HIP JOINT

Valves

PLUG-IN PANEL
FROM COMPUTER
(1950s)

Metal stem
fits into leg
bone.

ELECTRICITY AND ELECTRONICS
From light bulbs to computers, many
of the things that we use today
are powered by electricity
or controlled by electronics.

Mouthpiece
converts sound into
electrical signals.

Hook for
earpiece

COMMUNICATION
Information has
become one of the
most important
commodities in modern life.
Inventions such as the telephone
and the fax machine have helped
speed information across the
globe in an instant.

Earpiece converts
electrical signals
into sound.

Numbered dial
connects caller.

Wire

DIAL TELEPHONE
(c.1929)

# COUNTING AND COMPUTING

DEVICES THAT AID COUNTING have been around for thousands of years. About 5,000 years ago, the Mesopotamians recorded their calculations by sliding small stones along furrows in the ground – an idea similar to the abacus, which appeared later in China and Japan.

*Upper beads represent five times the value of lower beads.*

## ABACUS
Although it is the oldest calculating device, the abacus is still in use today. Numbers are recorded by moving the beads, which are arranged in rows representing units, tens, etc.

*Scales are used to multiply numbers.*

SLIDE RULE

## SLIDE RULE
Englishman William Oughtred invented the slide rule in about 1622. His device used John Napier's invention of logarithms, which transformed the tedious task of multiplication into addition.

BABBAGE'S DIFFERENCE ENGINE (1832)

## BABBAGE'S ENGINE
This machine, built in 1832 by Charles Babbage, was the first automatic calculator. Babbage went on to design a programmable machine, which unfortunately was never built.

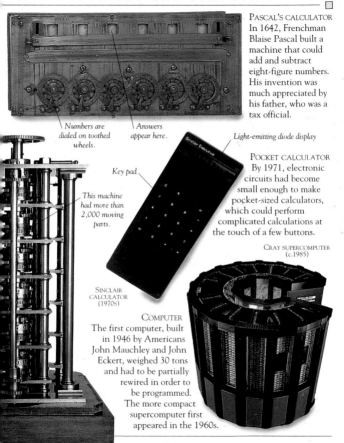

**PASCAL'S CALCULATOR**
In 1642, Frenchman Blaise Pascal built a machine that could add and subtract eight-figure numbers. His invention was much appreciated by his father, who was a tax official.

*Numbers are dialed on toothed wheels.*

*Answers appear here.*

*Light-emitting diode display*

*This machine had more than 2,000 moving parts.*

*Key pad*

**POCKET CALCULATOR**
By 1971, electronic circuits had become small enough to make pocket-sized calculators, which could perform complicated calculations at the touch of a few buttons.

CRAY SUPERCOMPUTER (c.1985)

SINCLAIR CALCULATOR (1970s)

**COMPUTER**
The first computer, built in 1946 by Americans John Mauchley and John Eckert, weighed 30 tons and had to be partially rewired in order to be programmed. The more compact supercomputer first appeared in the 1960s.

# OPTICAL INVENTIONS

MICROSCOPES, TELESCOPES, and other optical
inventions have been vital for advances in
science. Most optical devices contain lenses,
which can make small objects appear larger or
distant objects appear closer. Lenses
depend on the fact that rays
of light bend, or refract,
as they pass from
air to glass.

*Observer
looks here.*

*Sliding
focus*

## WATCHING THE STARS

The first telescope
was built in 1608 by
Dutchman Hans
Lippershey. It had
two lenses that
refracted the light
and made distant
objects look much
closer. A year
later, Italian
Galileo Galilei
used a similar
telescope to study
the Moon.

*Telescope
swivels on
wooden ball.*

NEWTON'S
REFLECTOR
(1668)

## MAGNIFYING WITH MIRRORS

In 1668, Isaac Newton built
the first reflecting telescope,
which used curved mirrors
instead of lenses to magnify
distant objects. It produced
much clearer images
than could be obtained
with refracting telescopes
of the time.

GALILEO'S
TELESCOPE
(EARLY 17TH
CENTURY)

## MAGNIFYING GLASS

Robert Grosseteste was the first to suggest using lenses to magnify small objects. His pupil, Roger Bacon, made the first magnifying glass in 1267.

MAGNIFYING GLASS
(17TH CENTURY)

Colored glass

Lens

Ribbons were attached here.

Lens holder

IRON-FRAMED
EYEGLASSES
(1750)

## EYEGLASSES

Made in Venice in about 1280, the first eyeglasses had convex (outward-curving) lenses and were suitable only for close-up vision.

## MICROSCOPE

The first compound microscope (with two or more lenses) was made in 1590 by Hans Janssen and his son, Zacharias. It enabled them to see tiny objects, invisible to the naked eye.

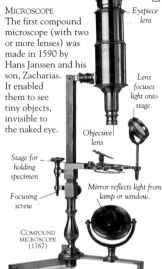

Eyepiece lens

Lens focuses light onto stage.

Objective lens

Stage for holding specimen

Focusing screw

Mirror reflects light from lamp or window.

COMPOUND
MICROSCOPE
(1767)

## SEEING DOUBLE?

Prisms reflect the light back on itself, lengthening its path.

Eyepiece lens

Binoculars use prisms (specially shaped blocks of glass) to reflect the light. Because the prisms send the light backward and forward, binoculars can be made much shorter than telescopes. The first "prismatic" binoculars were made in about 1880.

### OPTICAL FACTS

• People thought the Moon was smooth, until Galileo saw its craters through his telescope.

• Bifocal eyeglasses were invented in 1784 by Benjamin Franklin.

• Microscopic cells were first described by Robert Hooke in 1665.

# RECORDING THE WEATHER

METEOROLOGY, THE SCIENTIFIC study of the weather, began in Italy during the 17th century, when scientists started to devise instruments that could measure changes in the temperature, pressure, and moisture content of the air. Records about the weather could then be used to note patterns and make forecasts.

THERMOMETER
(18TH CENTURY)

Scale shows temperature.

Mercury bulb

WET AND DRY BULB THERMOMETER

In dry air, moisture in the muslin evaporates and cools the bulb.

Scale

Damp muslin

Dry bulb measures air temperature normally.

THERMOMETER
The mercury thermometer was devised by Gabriel Fahrenheit in 1714. As the air temperature rises, the mercury in the bulb expands and moves up the glass tube.

MEASURING HUMIDITY
Early humidity-measuring devices used human hair, which gets longer when it is damp. But the wet and dry bulb thermometer, devised by John Daniell in 1820, compares the temperature readings of a wet and a dry bulb to indicate the moisture content of the air.

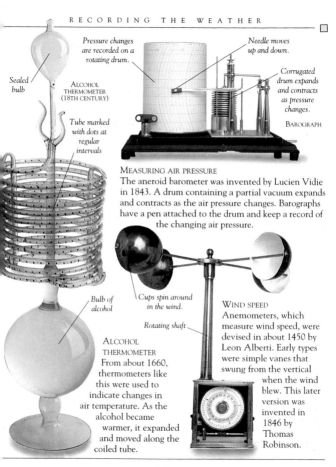

*Pressure changes are recorded on a rotating drum.*

*Needle moves up and down.*

*Sealed bulb*

ALCOHOL THERMOMETER (18TH CENTURY)

*Corrugated drum expands and contracts as pressure changes.*

BAROGRAPH

*Tube marked with dots at regular intervals*

MEASURING AIR PRESSURE

The aneroid barometer was invented by Lucien Vidie in 1843. A drum containing a partial vacuum expands and contracts as the air pressure changes. Barographs have a pen attached to the drum and keep a record of the changing air pressure.

*Bulb of alcohol*

*Cups spin around in the wind.*

*Rotating shaft*

ALCOHOL THERMOMETER

From about 1660, thermometers like this were used to indicate changes in air temperature. As the alcohol became warmer, it expanded and moved along the coiled tube.

WIND SPEED

Anemometers, which measure wind speed, were devised in about 1450 by Leon Alberti. Early types were simple vanes that swung from the vertical when the wind blew. This later version was invented in 1846 by Thomas Robinson.

# ELECTRICITY

IN 1752, AFTER FLYING his kite in a thunderstorm, American scientist Benjamin Franklin showed that lightning was a form of electricity. Franklin's work led to a huge interest in electrical science and paved the way for many new and exciting inventions and discoveries.

Glass rod

Zinc disk

Copper disk

LIGHTNING ROD (1750S)

Lightning rod discharges electricity into the ground.

Rod was attached to the highest point of building.

THE FIRST BATTERY
In 1800, Italian scientist Alessandro Volta made the first battery by piling up alternate copper and zinc disks separated by cloth pads soaked in weak acid. An electrochemical reaction between the disks generated a constant flow of electric charge.

LIGHTNING ROD
Franklin's experiments led him to invent the lightning rod in 1752. The rod was attached to the highest point of a building to prevent the building from being struck by lightning during thunderstorms.

Cloth pad soaked in salt water or weak acid

VOLTAIC PILE

Wooden base

ELECTRICITY AND MOVEMENT

In 1823, English scientist William Sturgeon made the first electromagnet by winding a wire around an iron rod. When a current flowed through the wire, the rod became magnetic. Eight years later, American scientist Joseph Henry used this effect to make one of the first electric motors.

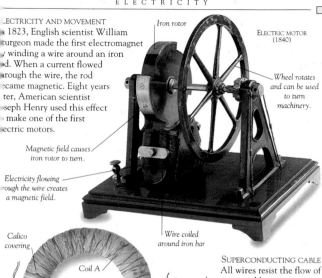

*Iron rotor*

ELECTRIC MOTOR
(1840)

*Wheel rotates and can be used to turn machinery.*

*Magnetic field causes iron rotor to turn.*

*Electricity flowing through the wire creates a magnetic field.*

*Wire coiled around iron bar*

*Calico covering*

Coil A

FARADAY'S RING
(1831)

Coil B

*Copper wire*

TRANSFORMER

In 1831, Michael Faraday made an iron ring with two separate wires coiled around it. A varying current in coil A induced a current in coil B, even though the two wires didn't touch. Without realizing it, Faraday had invented the transformer.

SUPERCONDUCTING CABLE

All wires resist the flow of electricity and lose some power as heat. In 1911, Dutch scientist Heike Onnes found that metals cooled to very low temperatures can become superconductors – in other words, they carry current much more efficiently.

*Liquid nitrogen cools the wires.*

*Vacuum keeps temperature low.*

# ELECTRONICS

TELEVISIONS, COMPUTERS, and many other gadgets that we use today are electronic. Electronics involves using special components to control electricity itself. Over the years, electronic components have become smaller and smaller, so that millions of electronic circuits can now be fitted into a tiny silicon chip.

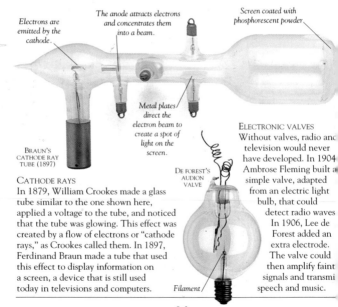

*Electrons are emitted by the cathode.*

*The anode attracts electrons and concentrates them into a beam.*

*Screen coated with phosphorescent powder.*

*Metal plates direct the electron beam to create a spot of light on the screen.*

BRAUN'S CATHODE RAY TUBE (1897)

DE FOREST'S AUDION VALVE

*Filament*

CATHODE RAYS
In 1879, William Crookes made a glass tube similar to the one shown here, applied a voltage to the tube, and noticed that the tube was glowing. This effect was created by a flow of electrons or "cathode rays," as Crookes called them. In 1897, Ferdinand Braun made a tube that used this effect to display information on a screen, a device that is still used today in televisions and computers.

ELECTRONIC VALVES
Without valves, radio and television would never have developed. In 1904 Ambrose Fleming built a simple valve, adapted from an electric light bulb, that could detect radio waves. In 1906, Lee de Forest added an extra electrode. The valve could then amplify faint signals and transmi speech and music.

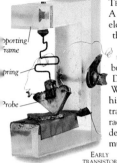

*Supporting frame*

*Spring*

*Probe*

## THE FIRST TRANSISTOR

A major breakthrough in electronics came with the invention of the transistor, which did the same job as the valve but was much smaller. Developed by American William Shockley and his team in 1947, the transistor was used in radios and other electronic devices, making them much more compact.

EARLY TRANSISTOR

### ELECTRONICS FACTS

• The electron was discovered in 1897 by British physicist J. J. Thomson.

• The first computers were huge – they contained up to 20,000 valves and often filled whole rooms.

• American Jack Kilby invented the microchip in 1959.

*Microchip*

## PRINTING A CIRCUIT

Electronic equipment had to be built laboriously by hand until German engineer Paul Eisler came up with the idea of printing the tiny circuits onto copper foil attached to plastic boards. Eisler patented the printed circuit board in 1943. Integrated circuits, or microchips, appeared 16 years later.

*Tracks connecting components*

CIRCUIT BOARD FROM SMALL COMPUTER

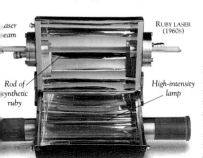

*Laser beam*

RUBY LASER (1960S)

*Rod of synthetic ruby*

*High-intensity lamp*

## LASERS

In 1960, Theodore Maiman made the first laser. He put a flash tube around a rod of ruby and produced a beam of laser light. Today lasers are used in all kinds of electronic devices, from supermarket scanners to compact disc players.

# HEALTH AND MEDICINE

DEVELOPMENTS IN SCIENCE and technology have led to many advances in health and medicine. Science helps researchers unravel the workings of the human body, while technology provides the tools with which doctors can treat their patients.

## Surgical inventions

Until the 19th century, surgical operations were often more life-threatening than the conditions they were supposed to cure. But techniques advanced rapidly during the 1800s, and the development of anesthetics, antiseptics, and new surgical tools meant that having an operation became a safer and less harrowing experience.

*Rubber tube*

*Valve lets ether vapor into rubber tube.*

*Valve draws air into the jar.*

*Sponges soaked in ether*

THE "LETHEON" ETHER INHALER (1847)

HARRINGTON'S CLOCKWORK DENTAL DRILL

*Winding key*

*Drill bit*

DRILLING AND FILLING
Englishman George Harrington devised a clockwork dental drill in 1863. When fully wound, the drill would keep going for up to two agonizing minutes.

## GERMFREE SURGERY

Developed by Joseph Lister in the 1860s, antiseptics reduced the risk of infection during surgery. Lister used a steam spray like this to spray the antiseptic around the operation site.

CARBOLIC STEAM SPRAY (1875)

*Mouthpiece*

## ANESTHETICS

In 1846, surgeons began to use ether and chloroform to make their patients unconscious before surgery. The inhaler ensured that only the patient was affected by the anesthetic.

*Porcelain teeth*

PARTIAL DENTURES (c.1860)

*Coiled spring*

## FALSE TEETH

In 1774, Frenchman Alexis Duchâteau devised the first well-fitting set of false teeth. His partner added springs, which kept the false teeth in place.

---

### SURGICAL FACTS

• In prehistoric times, holes were drilled in people's skulls as a treatment for insanity.

• In about 700 B.C., the Etruscan people of southern Europe wore dentures made from animal teeth.

• In medieval times, surgery was often performed by barbers.

---

*Wire to heart*

*Pulse generator*

## SETTING THE PACE

In 1952, American doctor Paul Zoll used electrical impulses to revive a failing heart. This led to the invention of the pacemaker, which is inserted next to the patient's heart and automatically ensures a regular beat.

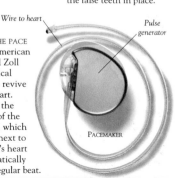

PACEMAKER

# Investigative medicine

Surgery can be risky and expensive, so it is important for doctors to be able to find out what is going on inside a patient's body without operating. Investigative techniques are quicker and less painful than surgery and can be used as part of a patient's treatment as well as for checking general health.

NURSING THE SICK

FEELING FEVERISH?
A body temperature just one or two degrees above normal is a sure sign that something is wrong. Thanks to the clinical thermometer, developed by Thomas Allbut in 1866, people can take their own temperature without going to a doctor.

*Temperature scale*

*Curved thermometer is placed under patient's armpit.*

*Mercury bulb*

THERMOMETERS
(c.1865)

*Funnel concentrates the light.*

*Candle provides light.*

*Speculum is placed in patient's ear.*

ENDOSCOPE
(1880s)

*Viewing lenses*

LOOKING INSIDE
Nineteenth-century physicians used gadgets like this to look inside patients' ears and other awkward places. The modern, flexible endoscope, first made by American Basil Hirschovitz in 1957, uses optical fibers to reach farther with less discomfort.

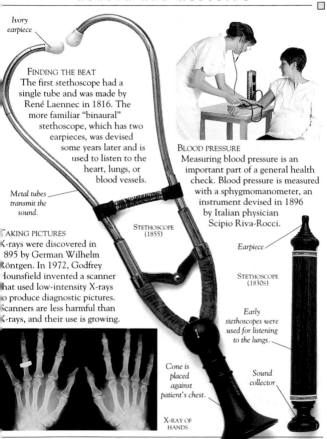

*Ivory earpiece*

FINDING THE BEAT
The first stethoscope had a single tube and was made by René Laennec in 1816. The more familiar "binaural" stethoscope, which has two earpieces, was devised some years later and is used to listen to the heart, lungs, or blood vessels.

*Metal tubes transmit the sound.*

STETHOSCOPE
(1855)

TAKING PICTURES
X-rays were discovered in 1895 by German Wilhelm Röntgen. In 1972, Godfrey Hounsfield invented a scanner that used low-intensity X-rays to produce diagnostic pictures. Scanners are less harmful than X-rays, and their use is growing.

BLOOD PRESSURE
Measuring blood pressure is an important part of a general health check. Blood pressure is measured with a sphygmomanometer, an instrument devised in 1896 by Italian physician Scipio Riva-Rocci.

*Earpiece*

STETHOSCOPE
(1830s)

*Early stethoscopes were used for listening to the lungs.*

*Sound collector*

*Cone is placed against patient's chest.*

X-RAY OF
HANDS

# COMMUNICATION

THE ABILITY TO COMMUNICATE is essential to our everyday lives. Early people conveyed information by word of mouth or by signaling to each other with fires or lights. But as civilizations developed, many new and ingenious ways of passing on information were invented.

## Writing

Writing is one of the oldest forms of communication. The first written signs may have developed as a way for traders to keep records of their transactions. Early writing was inscribed on clay or stone using flints and sticks. Paper, inks, and an array of writing implements developed later.

EARLY WRITING
Cuneiform, the first true system of writing, was devised in Mesopotamia more than 5,000 years ago. The wedge-shaped symbols were pressed into wet clay with sharpened sticks.

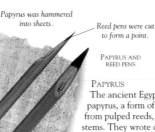

*Papyrus was hammered into sheets.*

*Reed pens were cut to form a point.*

PAPYRUS AND REED PENS

PAPYRUS
The ancient Egyptians invented papyrus, a form of paper made from pulped reeds, or plant stems. They wrote on the papyrus with reed pens and with ink made from water, soot, and natural gum.

*Sharpened point*

Nib

## WRITING FACTS

- Paper was invented in China in A.D. 105.

- Steel pen points, or nibs, appeared in 1829 but were not common until 40 years later.

- Early inks were made from natural plant dyes.

- Ballpoint pens were popular with pilots, who used them for writing at high altitudes.

QUILL PEN
Feathers were first used as pens in around 500 B.C. Because of the way they curve, left wing feathers proved to be more suitable for right-handed people, and vice-versa.

FEATHER QUILL

*Feathers from large birds have wide shafts that are easy to hold.*

*Hollow shaft, or quill*

FOUNTAIN PEN
The fountain pen made it possible to write without constantly reinking the pen. Ink is held in a reservoir inside the pen and flows through the nib to the paper.

*Lever for filling fountain pen with ink*

FOUNTAIN PEN

*Ink tube*

*Spring*

ON THE BALL
Lazlo Biro devised the first successful ballpoint pen in 1938. A narrow tube just above the free-moving ball provides a gentle flow of ink onto the paper. The ball also keeps air out when the pen is not in use, so the ink doesn't dry up.

*Ball*

BALLPOINT PEN

# Printing

Before printing, every book had to be written out by hand. This meant that books were rare, expensive, and available only to wealthy people. One of the pioneers of printing was the German, Johannes Gutenberg, whose ingenuity enabled books to be produced in large numbers for the first time.

### THE FIRST PRINTERS

Book-printing began during the 6th century in Japan and China, where handcarved wooden blocks were used to print individual pages. A steady hand was essential; one mistake meant the whole block would have to be carved again.

JAPANESE WOODEN PRINTING BLOCK

### TYPECASTING

In 1450, Gutenberg invented movable type – single letters that could be set in lines and reused. He carved letters to make molds, poured hot metal into the molds to make the type, and then set the type on a tray ready for printing.

Hard metal punch used to make mold

Mold used to make piece of type

HAND PRESS
(17TH CENTURY)

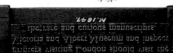

Individual pieces of type arranged in reverse

Tray

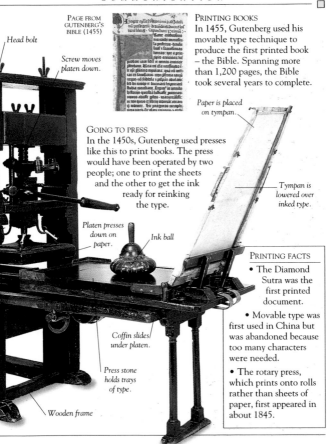

PAGE FROM
GUTENBERG'S
BIBLE (1455)

## PRINTING BOOKS

In 1455, Gutenberg used his movable type technique to produce the first printed book – the Bible. Spanning more than 1,200 pages, the Bible took several years to complete.

Head bolt

Screw moves platen down.

Paper is placed on tympan.

## GOING TO PRESS

In the 1450s, Gutenberg used presses like this to print books. The press would have been operated by two people; one to print the sheets and the other to get the ink ready for reinking the type.

Tympan is lowered over inked type.

Platen presses down on paper.

Ink ball

Coffin slides under platen.

Press stone holds trays of type.

Wooden frame

## PRINTING FACTS

• The Diamond Sutra was the first printed document.

• Movable type was first used in China but was abandoned because too many characters were needed.

• The rotary press, which prints onto rolls rather than sheets of paper, first appeared in about 1845.

# Postal services

Before the development of organized postal systems, letters and packages had to be delivered personally or via messengers. The Romans were among the first to have an official mail service, but it wasn't until the 1850s that prepaid mail could simply be dropped in a mailbox and delivered to almost anywhere in the world.

EARLY MAILBOX

### MAILING A LETTER

Mailboxes save people a trip to the post office. The first mailbox was set up in Guernsey, in the English Channel, in 1852. Staff from the local post office collected the mail at regular intervals during the day.

*Stamps were invented as proof that the postage has been paid.*

POSTAGE STAMPS

### POSTAGE STAMPS

People used to pay for their mail when it was delivered rather than before it was sent. But Englishman Rowland Hill came up with the idea of paying for postage in advance, and the first postage stamps were introduced in 1840.

ON THE MOVE
The introduction of trains with sorting cars in 1838 made next-day postal deliveries possible. The mail was sorted while the train was on the move.

MAIL FACTS
• Early sorting cars had hooks and chutes so mailbags could be picked up and dropped without stopping.

• Automatic sorting is up to 10 times faster than manual sorting.

• Despite the fear of plane crashes, air-mail was adopted widely in 1911.

SENDING GREETINGS
Postcards provide a quick and easy way to send a message. They are thought to have originated during the 1860s in either the US or Austria and were in widespread use by the 1870s.

*Message is written on the other side.*

POST CARD

*Address is written here.*

*Sorted mail*

*Operator types zip code into keyboard.*

SORTING AT SPEED
Introduced in the US in the 1960s, automatic sorting speeds up the sorting process. The operator punches the zip codes into a keyboard, and the letters are sorted by the machine.

# Keeping in touch

The invention of the telegraph and the telephone in the 19th century meant that written and verbal messages could be sent quickly over long distances for the first time. Today, people on opposite sides of the globe can talk to each other at the touch of a few buttons.

ABC TELEGRAPH (1837)

Magnetic needles

GETTING THE MESSAGE
Early telegraphs could send messages only in coded form. But in 1837, British inventors William Cooke and Charles Wheatstone demonstrated a telegraph that could both send and receive messages letter by letter. Messages were spelled out by magnetic needles, which pointed to individual letters.

*Incoming messages are spelled out by magnetic needles.*

*Outgoing messages are tapped out on buttons.*

Wire carrying signal from mouthpiece to receiver

Diaphragm

Mouthpiece

Earpiece

Mouthpiece

**TELEPHONE**
Alexander Graham Bell invented the telephone in 1876. Telephones like the one shown here, which worked as both the mouthpiece and the receiver, were in use shortly afterward.

Wire

**DIALING A NUMBER**
Before dial telephones were invented, all calls went via an operator. US undertaker Almon Strowger devised the first dial telephone in 1889, after discovering that operators were taking bribes to divert business calls to his competitors.

Numbered dial connects caller via automatic exchange.

Coils of wire inside the case carry messages as pulses of electricity.

Liquid crystal display

Numbered buttons are pressed on a keypad.

Earpiece

**ON THE MOVE**
The mobile phone means that telephones no longer need to be tied down by wires. The idea originated in the 1940s at the Bell Telephone Laboratories in the US, but the technology was not available to set up a public service until 30 years later.

# In the office

In order to survive and grow, businesses need to be able to communicate quickly and efficiently. Office mechanization began in 1874 with the introduction of the Remington typewriter. Since then, the arrival of photocopiers, fax machines, and other devices has made office tasks much easier.

*Reel holding magnetic wire*

POULSEN'S TELEGRAPHONE

*Carriage return moves paper up to next line.*

*Keys*

TAKING MESSAGES
In 1898, Valdemar Poulsen invented the first magnetic voice recorder. It was designed to record conversations so that people couldn't duck out of verbal agreements made over the phone.

TYPEWRITER
Until the invention of the typewriter, all documents were written out by hand. The "QWERTY" keyboard, which has the most often-used letters spaced apart to prevent jamming, was devised by Christopher Scholes in 1873.

*QWERTY keyboard*

XEROX COPIER
(c.1950)

*Early copiers were hand-operated.*

Charging chamber

Plate attracts toner.

## SENDING A FAX
The idea of sending images down a wire was patented by Scotsman Alexander Bain in 1843. Huge facsimile machines were later used by newspapers to send pictures around the world, but it wasn't until the 1980s that fax machines became small enough for office use.

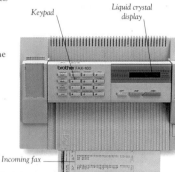

Keypad

Liquid crystal display

## TAKING A COPY
Photocopiers use electrostatic charge to attract black powder (toner) onto the paper. The photocopier was invented in 1938 by American lawyer Chester Carlson, who wanted to copy patent documents quickly and cleanly.

Incoming fax

MODERN FAX MACHINE

Screen

Computer

Keyboard

Mouse

## WORD PROCESSOR
In many of today's offices, typewriters have been replaced by word processors, which enable text to be stored and corrections to be made easily. The first word processor, devised by the IBM company in 1964, was the size of a desk and had no screen. Modern word processors are simply personal computers coupled with printers.

# TRAVEL AND EXPLORATION

# INTRODUCTION

THE DESIRE TO TRAVEL by land, sea, or air has inspired many great inventions. From bicycles to biplanes, hundreds of different forms of transportation have been devised. The development of sailing ships and navigation led to worldwide exploration, travel, and trade.

GLOBE

FACILE BICYCLE
(1888)

NAVIGATION
Travelers and explorers once depended on maps and globes to navigate long journeys, but advances in electronics have now made traveling safer and easier.

*Pedals attached to front wheel*

BICYCLES
A relative newcomer in the history of unpowered transportation, the bicycle has evolved into one of the most efficient machines ever devised.

*Passenger's seat*

MOTOR CARS
The first motor car was built in the late 1800s. In just over a century, the car has changed from an expensive and unreliable "horseless carriage" into an everyday form of transportation used by millions of people all over the world.

*This car had a top speed of 4 mph (6 km/h).*

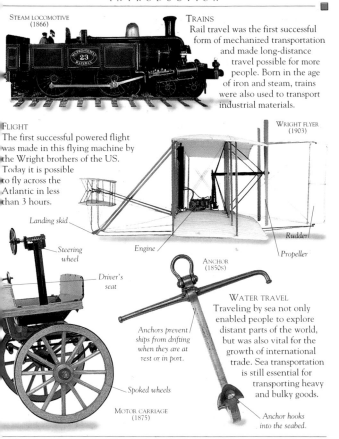

STEAM LOCOMOTIVE
(1866)

## TRAINS
Rail travel was the first successful
form of mechanized transportation
and made long-distance
travel possible for more
people. Born in the age
of iron and steam, trains
were also used to transport
industrial materials.

## FLIGHT
The first successful powered flight
was made in this flying machine by
the Wright brothers of the US.
Today it is possible
to fly across the
Atlantic in less
than 3 hours.

WRIGHT FLYER
(1903)

Landing skid

Steering
wheel

Engine

Rudder

Propeller

Driver's
seat

ANCHOR
(1850s)

Anchors prevent
ships from drifting
when they are at
rest or in port.

## WATER TRAVEL
Traveling by sea not only
enabled people to explore
distant parts of the world,
but was also vital for the
growth of international
trade. Sea transportation
is still essential for
transporting heavy
and bulky goods.

Spoked wheels

MOTOR CARRIAGE
(1875)

Anchor hooks
into the seabed.

# WHEELS AND EARLY VEHICLES

DEVISED IN MESOPOTAMIA more than 5,000 years ago, the wheel is one of the most important inventions of all time. As well as being vital for the development of transportation, wheels were used by potters for turning clay and became essential components of later inventions, such as steam engines and clocks.

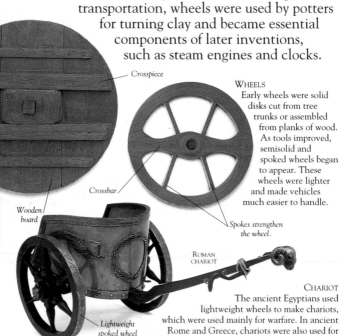

Crosspiece

Crossbar

Wooden board

### WHEELS

Early wheels were solid disks cut from tree trunks or assembled from planks of wood. As tools improved, semisolid and spoked wheels began to appear. These wheels were lighter and made vehicles much easier to handle.

Spokes strengthen the wheel.

ROMAN CHARIOT

Lightweight spoked wheel

### CHARIOT

The ancient Egyptians used lightweight wheels to make chariots, which were used mainly for warfare. In ancient Rome and Greece, chariots were also used for racing, a popular form of entertainment.

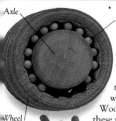

Axle

Roller bearings enable wheel to turn freely.

Wheel

Roller bearings

### WHEEL BEARINGS

Bearings were invented to reduce the friction between the axle and the wheel so that the wheel turned more easily. Wooden roller bearings like these were probably devised by Danish wagonmakers in about 100 B.C.

### WHEEL FACTS

• In some early carts, the axle was fixed to the wheels and rotated as the wheels turned.

• Carriage wheels had to be oiled daily until the invention of the self-oiling axle in 1787.

• Before springs were added, carriages were suspended from straps.

CARRIAGE SPRING

Metal bands hold layers of steel together.

Layers (or "leaves") of steel

### A SMOOTHER RIDE

Elliptical (or oval-shaped) springs were devised by Obadiah Elliot in 1805 and used on horse-drawn carriages to give a smoother ride.

When the carriage hit a bump, the leaves of steel would bend and then spring back into shape.

HORSE-DRAWN CARRIAGE

Spring attached to the body of the carriage

# HORSE POWER

HORSES WERE USED as pack animals as long ago as 4500 B.C. and were first ridden about 2,000 years later. Saddles and bridles made horses easier to ride and control, but it wasn't until the invention of the padded collar that horses could be used to pull carriages, carts, and other heavy loads.

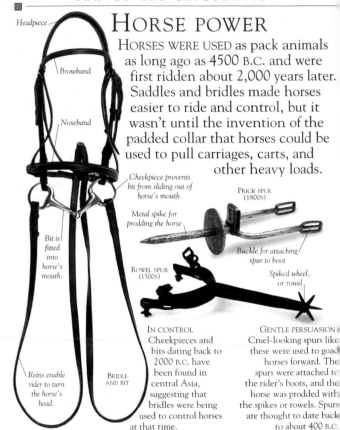

*Headpiece*

*Browband*

*Noseband*

*Cheekpiece prevents bit from sliding out of horse's mouth.*

*Bit is fitted into horse's mouth.*

*Reins enable rider to turn the horse's head.*

BRIDLE AND BIT

PRICK SPUR (1800s)

*Metal spike for prodding the horse*

*Buckle for attaching spur to boot*

ROWEL SPUR (1500s)

*Spiked wheel, or rowel*

IN CONTROL Cheekpieces and bits dating back to 2000 B.C. have been found in central Asia, suggesting that bridles were being used to control horses at that time.

GENTLE PERSUASION Cruel-looking spurs like these were used to goad horses forward. The spurs were attached to the rider's boots, and the horse was prodded with the spikes or rowels. Spurs are thought to date back to about 400 B.C.

HIPPOSANDAL

## FOOTWEAR

The Romans used iron "hipposandals" to protect their horses' feet on rough or stony ground. Hoof-shaped shoes, which appeared in Europe in about A.D. 800 and are still used today, are more practical for traveling quickly.

*Horse's hoof fits on flat surface.*

*Loop for attaching strap*

*Ornate fretwork*

*Pommel*

## SADDLE

The invention of the saddle led to a safer and more comfortable journey, both for the rider and the horse. The first saddles, little more than rugs, were used in Siberia from about 600 B.C.

*Seat*

TIBETAN SADDLE
(18TH CENTURY)

CHINESE STIRRUP (1800S)

*Stirrup hangs from the saddle.*

*Rider's foot is placed here.*

## STIRRUPS

Stirrups were invented in Asia and spread to China in the 5th century. They had a big impact on warfare because they helped horsemen to balance more easily as they brandished their weapons.

## PULLING A LOAD

Early attempts to get horses to pull heavy loads failed because the harnesses used caused the horses to choke. The rigid padded collar, which fits around the horse's neck, was invented so that horses could pull heavy loads while breathing normally.

# WATER TRAVEL

FOR CENTURIES, PEOPLE have tried to find new ways to travel on water. After discovering how to harness the wind, early explorers and travelers took to the seas in simple sailboats. The invention of the steam engine and the arrival of new shipbuilding materials led to bigger and faster vessels that dominated long-distance travel until the jet age.

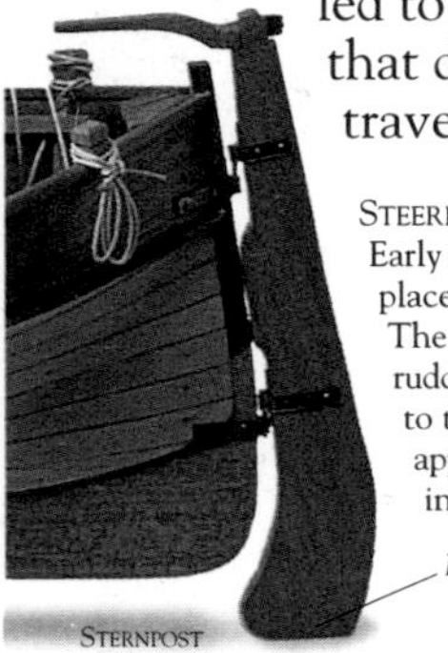

### STEERING STRAIGHT
Early ships were steered with an oar placed over the side of the vessel. The more effective sternpost rudder, which was attached to the back of the boat, appeared in Europe in about 1200.

*Rudder blade*

**STERNPOST RUDDER**

### SAILS AND RIGGING
The first sailboats had square sails and always traveled in the direction of the wind. Triangular lateen sails, invented in 200 B.C., enabled boats to sail against the wind.

*Lateen sail*

**LATEEN SAILBOAT**

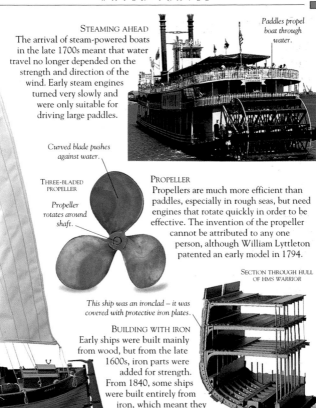

### STEAMING AHEAD

The arrival of steam-powered boats in the late 1700s meant that water travel no longer depended on the strength and direction of the wind. Early steam engines turned very slowly and were only suitable for driving large paddles.

*Paddles propel boat through water.*

*Curved blade pushes against water.*

THREE-BLADED PROPELLER

*Propeller rotates around shaft.*

### PROPELLER

Propellers are much more efficient than paddles, especially in rough seas, but need engines that rotate quickly in order to be effective. The invention of the propeller cannot be attributed to any one person, although William Lyttleton patented an early model in 1794.

SECTION THROUGH HULL OF HMS WARRIOR

*This ship was an ironclad – it was covered with protective iron plates.*

### BUILDING WITH IRON

Early ships were built mainly from wood, but from the late 1600s, iron parts were added for strength. From 1840, some ships were built entirely from iron, which meant they were stronger and lighter and could carry heavier loads.

# RAILROAD TRAVEL

LONG BEFORE THE FIRST locomotives
were built, wagons carrying heavy loads
were hauled along tracks by humans
or horses. But with the invention
of the steam engine came the first
self-propelled trains, which were
to revolutionize travel all
over the world.

*"Home"*
(stop)
signal

*"Distant"*
(warning)
signal

### SIGNALS
Signals are essential if
two or more trains use the
same track. Semaphore
signals like this were first
used in the 1840s.
The upper arm tells
the driver to stop; the
lower arm tells the driver
to prepare to stop at the
next signal.

— Chimney

Boiler          Piston

*Arm drives
the wheels.*

*Footplate*

MECHANICAL
SEMAPHORE SIGNAL

### STEAM LOCOMOTIVE
The world's first steam
locomotive, built by
British inventor Richard
Trevithick, ran in 1804.
The engine pulled
a train carrying 70
people over a distance
of 10 miles (16 km).

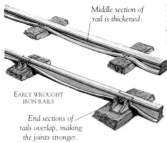

*Middle section of rail is thickened.*

EARLY WROUGHT IRON RAILS

*End sections of rails overlap, making the joints stronger.*

## MAKING TRACKS

Early rails were made of cast iron and often broke under the strain of heavy locomotives. Gradually, these rails were replaced by stronger wrought iron tracks. Steel rails, which are stronger still, appeared in 1857.

## DIESEL POWER

Invented in 1892, the diesel engine generates electricity, which can be used to turn the wheels of a train. The first diesel-electric locomotive ran in 1923.

DELTIC DIESEL-ELECTRIC LOCOMOTIVE (1956)

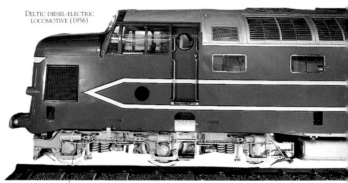

*Wheels are driven by electric motors.*

## MAGLEV TRAINS

During the 1950s, British engineer Eric Laithwaite developed a motor that could suspend a train above the tracks by magnetic levitation. Although currently used only on a small scale, these Maglev trains may become the trains of the future.

# PEDAL POWER

BICYCLING IS ONE of the simplest and cheapest ways to travel. Invented about 200 years ago, the first bicycles required great skill and courage to ride. But the addition of steering, pedals, and brakes made bicycling a much less dangerous form of transportation.

A BICYCLE MADE FOR TWO

## BEFORE PEDALS
The hobby horse was the forerunner of the bicycle. It consisted of a wooden beam set above two spoked wheels. The rider would sit astride the machine and push the ground with alternate feet. German Baron Karl von Drais produced a machine with steering in 1818.

Bar on which rider rested his or her chest

Handle bars

Seat

*Rubber coating*    *Strips of sailcloth*

DUNLOP'S TIRE

*Inner tube filled with air*

Wooden beam

## RIDING ON AIR
Pneumatic (air-filled) tires were originally invented by William Thomson in 1845. But they didn't become popular until 1888, when John Dunlop revived them to help his son win a bicycle race.

The front wheel could be steered.

HOBBY HORSE (1820s)

*Pedal*

DERAILLEUR GEARS

*Large cog turns wheels slowly.*

*Small cog turns wheels quickly.*

*Chain*

### CHANGING GEAR

Bicycling uphill became much easier after the addition of derailleur gears in 1896. Gears enable the wheels to turn at different speeds while the cyclist pedals normally.

### BICYCLE FACTS

• Derailleur gears were patented by Englishman Edmund Hodgkinson.

• The hobby horse could reach a speed of 10 mph (16 km/h).

• In 1839, Kirkpatrick Macmillan committed the first cycling offense when he hit a child with his bicycle.

### SAFETY FIRST

During the 1870s, bicycles with huge front wheels became popular, but were dangerous to ride. In 1885, John Starley devised the safety bicycle, which had equal-sized wheels with the saddle in between.

STARLEY'S SAFETY BICYCLE (1885)

*Spoked iron wheel*

*Strong, lightweight steel tubing*

*Thicker tubing and decorative lugs strengthen the joints.*

### IMPROVING THE FRAME

In 1898, A. Reynolds patented a way of making steel tubing that was light and strong – ideal for bicycle frames. The tubing was thin for most of its length and thicker at the ends.

# ON THE ROAD

A FEW STEAM-POWERED vehicles ran in the early 1800s, but they were too heavy for road use. It was after the arrival of the internal combustion engine, invented by Etienne Lenoir and improved by Nikolaus Otto, that the first motor cars were built.

STEAM-POWERED
MOTORCYCLE
(1889)

## STEAM POWER

Compact steam engines were used in several small road vehicles until about 1910. The first motorcycle, made by the Michaux brothers of France, was in fact steam-powered.

## THE FIRST CAR

The first car to be sold to the public was made in 1885 by German Karl Benz. The engine was at the back of the car and powered the rear wheels. By 1896, more than 130 cars had been built at the Benz factory.

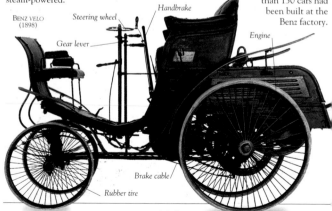

BENZ VELO
(1898)

*Steering wheel*

*Handbrake*

*Gear lever*

*Engine*

*Brake cable*

*Rubber tire*

### CAT'S EYES

One foggy night in 1933, Percy Shaw nearly drove off the edge of the road, but was stopped by the reflection from the eyes of a cat. Shaw went on to invent the cat's-eye reflecting roadstud.

MODERN CAT'S-EYE ROADSTUD

*Beads reflect light from car headlights.*

### TRAFFIC LIGHTS

The first traffic lights, installed in Cleveland, Ohio in 1914, had only red and green lights. The yellow light was added four years later, and the design is now used all over the world.

### RADIAL-PLY TIRES

The arrival of pneumatic tires in the 1890s made traveling by road more comfortable than on previous solid rubber tires. In 1949, the Michelin company used radial plies – lengths of wire wound around the tread – to reinforce the rubber. Radial-ply tires last longer and grip the road better than their predecessors.

*Radial plies*

*Brake disk*

*Caliper houses pads, which are squeezed against the brake disk.*

### DISK BRAKES

Patented in 1902 by English carmaker Frederick Lanchester, disk brakes are now fitted to all cars. When the brakes are applied, friction pads squeeze the disk and the car slows down.

# PIONEERING FLIGHT

SINCE ANCIENT TIMES, the dream of flying has kept many inventors busy. Over the years, brave men and women have tried out an array of flying machines, many of which never left the ground. The first successful flight took place in 1783, when the Montgolfier brothers' hot-air balloon took to the skies.

MONTGOLFIER BALLOON

*Passengers' gallery*

### HOT AIR
Thousands of people watched as the Montgolfier balloon rose into the sky above Paris. The hot air was produced by a straw-burning fire at the mouth of the balloon.

### FLYING FACTS
• Helicopters were first proposed by Leonardo da Vinci in the 1400s.

• On its first flight, the Montgolfier balloon carried a duck, a sheep, and a rooster.

• In 1930, Amy Johnson became the first woman to fly solo from England to Australia.

### THE WRIGHT FLYER
In 1903, American bicycle makers Orville and Wilbur Wright built and flew the first powered airplane. Their *Flyer* was driven by a lightweight gasoline engine and flew a distance of half a mile (800 m).

*The rudder controls the direction of the plane.*

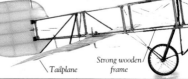

*Tailplane*

*Strong wooden frame*

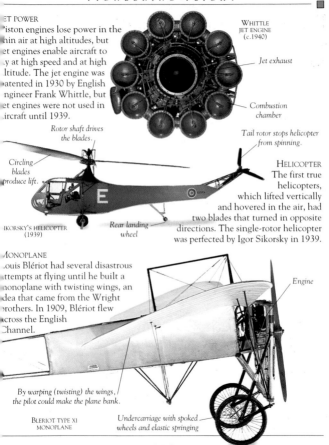

## JET POWER

Piston engines lose power in the thin air at high altitudes, but jet engines enable aircraft to fly at high speed and at high altitude. The jet engine was patented in 1930 by English engineer Frank Whittle, but jet engines were not used in aircraft until 1939.

WHITTLE JET ENGINE (c.1940)

Jet exhaust

Combustion chamber

Rotor shaft drives the blades.

Circling blades produce lift.

Tail rotor stops helicopter from spinning.

## HELICOPTER

The first true helicopters, which lifted vertically and hovered in the air, had two blades that turned in opposite directions. The single-rotor helicopter was perfected by Igor Sikorsky in 1939.

SIKORSKY'S HELICOPTER (1939)

Rear landing wheel

## MONOPLANE

Louis Blériot had several disastrous attempts at flying until he built a monoplane with twisting wings, an idea that came from the Wright brothers. In 1909, Blériot flew across the English Channel.

Engine

By warping (twisting) the wings, the pilot could make the plane bank.

BLÉRIOT TYPE XI MONOPLANE

Undercarriage with spoked wheels and elastic springing

# THE JET AGE AND SPACE TRAVEL

MODERN TECHNOLOGY has not only made worldwide air travel possible, but has also made the exploration of space a reality. Scientists believe that the aircraft of the future will make use of space technology by traveling in a semiorbit around the world.

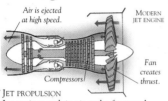

*Air is ejected at high speed.*

MODERN JET ENGINE

*Fan creates thrust.*

*Compressors*

JET PROPULSION
Jet engines suck in air at the front and eject it at high speed from the back. Spinning blades inside the engine raise the pressure of the air. As the air rushes backward, the engine is forced forward.

LIFT-OFF
The Saturn V space rocket was developed in the 1960s in order to send astronauts to the Moon. Because there is no air in space, scientists had to devise special oxygen-rich fuel to power the rocket.

*Fuel tanks*

SUPERSONIC FLIGHT
Concorde is the only supersonic passenger aircraft. It made its first flight in 1969 and now travels routinely at twice the speed of sound. Concorde can fly from New York to London in less than 3 hours.

## SPACE SHUTTLE

Launched by a huge rocket that is later abandoned in space, the Space Shuttle can orbit and then land like an ordinary aircraft. It first flew into space in 1981.

### SPACE FACTS

• In 1961, Soviet Yuri Gagarin became the first person to travel into space.

• Suits worn by shuttle astronauts weigh 227 lb (103 kg) on Earth but are weightless in space.

• Saturn V used 13.6 tons of fuel per second on takeoff.

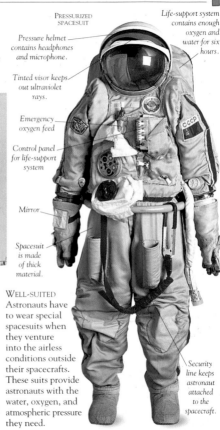

PRESSURIZED SPACESUIT

*Pressure helmet contains headphones and microphone.*

*Tinted visor keeps out ultraviolet rays.*

*Emergency oxygen feed*

*Control panel for life-support system*

*Mirror*

*Spacesuit is made of thick material.*

*Life-support system contains enough oxygen and water for six hours.*

*Security line keeps astronaut attached to the spacecraft.*

### WELL-SUITED

Astronauts have to wear special spacesuits when they venture into the airless conditions outside their spacecrafts. These suits provide astronauts with the water, oxygen, and atmospheric pressure they need.

# NAVIGATION

LONG-DISTANCE TRAVEL was unpredictable before navigating instruments were invented. Pioneering explorers had to rely on landmarks, or the position of the stars and planets, in order to work out where they were and to plan their journeys.

*Directions are marked on compass card.*

MAGNETIC COMPASS (1700s)

*Pivot*

*Reflector sends out and detects radio waves.*

*Octants measure the angle between the horizon and the Sun, Moon, or stars.*

OCTANT (c.1750)

*Central arm moves around pivot.*

*Graduated angle scale*

*Reading marker*

## MAGNETIC COMPASS

Early navigators found their way using lodestones – pieces of magnetic iron that hung from threads and always pointed north-south. Compasses were made by attaching the center points of these magnets to pieces of card marked with directions.

## OCTANTS AND SEXTANTS

Invented independently by Thomas Godfrey and John Hadley in 1731, the octant allowed explorers to work out their latitude. It was superseded by the sextant which, together with charts and a clock, measured longitude as well.

## MERCATOR PROJECTION MAP

Because they didn't show the effect of the Earth's curved surface, early maps tended to distort distances and directions. In 1569, Gerardus Kremer (known as Mercator) used a special projection technique to draw more accurate maps.

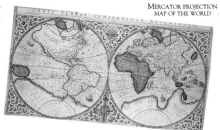

MERCATOR PROJECTION MAP OF THE WORLD

AIRFIELD RADAR (1953)

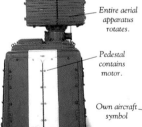

## RADAR

Introduced in the late 1930s, radar is vital for both air and water travel. By reflecting radio waves from solid objects, radar enables pilots to "see" obstacles at night or in misty conditions.

Entire aerial apparatus rotates.

Pedestal contains motor.

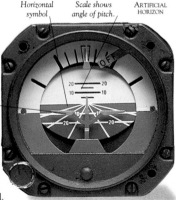

Horizontal symbol

Scale shows angle of pitch.

ARTIFICIAL HORIZON

Own aircraft symbol

## ON THE LEVEL

Flying aircraft through clouds can confuse even the most experienced pilots. In 1929, Elmer Sperry devised the artificial horizon, which shows the pilot whether the plane is level.

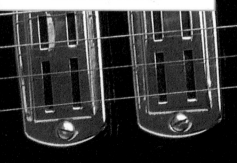

# ENTERTAINMENT AND LEISURE

# INTRODUCTION

OVER THE CENTURIES, various forms of entertainment and leisure have evolved. Until a hundred years ago, people made their own entertainment, or went out to hear music or see a play. But advances in science and technology have allowed the development of various new types of entertainment, many of which can be brought into people's homes.

### ENJOYING MUSIC
For thousands of years, people have enjoyed both making and listening to music. This pastime has led to a huge variety of musical instruments and an equally vast range of musical styles.

PORTUGUESE LUTE (1880s)

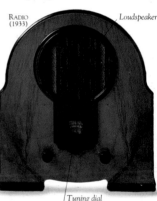

RADIO (1933)

Loudspeaker

CYLINDER RECORDER (c.1905)

Horn

Sounds are stored on drum.

Tuning dial

### RECORDING
Listening to recorded sounds became possible in 1877, when Thomas Edison devised a way of storing sounds onto a rotating cylinder.

### RADIO
Around 1915, a number of inventions made it possible to transmit speech and music. By the early 1920s, eager "wireless" listeners were tuning in to the first regular radio broadcasts.

### TELEVISION

In 1936, when television was first broadcast regularly, critics thought it wouldn't interest people for very long. But within less than half a century, television had become one of the most popular sources of entertainment.

### MOVIES

The invention of the magic lantern and other image projectors led to the growth of the movie theater. After the arrival of "talkies" (films with soundtracks) in 1927, the movie industry boomed.

MAGIC LANTERN (1908)

*Projection lens*

*Slide holder*

*Counters*

*Viewing window for acetylene lamp or candle*

BACKGAMMON SET (EARLY 1800S)

### PLAYING GAMES

Much ingenuity has gone into the invention of different games and toys. Many games, such as backgammon or chess, can be traced back hundreds or thousands of years. Others, such as electronic and video games, are much more recent inventions.

# SOUND AND VISION

MUCH OF OUR ENTERTAINMENT today involves listening to music, going to the movies, or watching television. Thanks to advances in technology, sounds can now be stored on disk or sent through the airwaves, while moving pictures can cross the globe in an instant.

*Fingerholes*

SUDANESE WHISTLE

## Musical instruments

Music-making is one of the oldest forms of entertainment. Since the first whistles appeared about 40,000 years ago, thousands of different musical instruments have evolved.

*Strings*

*Pickup converts the sound into electrical signals.*

*Hollow soundbox*

STRINGS AND BOWS
Bowed fiddles date back to the 10th century. As the bow moves across the strings, the strings vibrate and produce a sound.

*Bow*

*Strings*

IRANIAN SPIKE FIDDLE (1700s)

ELECTRIC GUITAR
In 1932, Adolphus Rickenbacker built the first electric guitar. His instrument was based on a traditional Spanish design.

*Control knobs for tone and volume*

RICKENBACKER ELECTRO-ACOUSTIC GUITAR (EARLY 1930S)

## PIANO

First built by Bartolomeo Cristofori in 1709, the piano was one of the first keyboard instruments that could play both softly and loudly, depending on how hard the keys were hit.

*Fingerboard*

*Pegs are turned to tune the strings.*

INSIDE A PIANO  \Strings

\Hammers strike the strings with varying force.

*The control panel enables sounds to be varied.*

ELECTRONIC KEYBOARD  *Display panel*

## ELECTRONIC SOUNDS

Popularized by Robert Moog in the 1970s, electronic synthesizers can produce a wide range of musical sounds at the touch of a few buttons.

*Each cymbal is a thin disk made of copper and tin.*

Leather strap  CYMBALS

## CLASHING CYMBALS

Cymbals have been played since ancient times. These cymbals were made by Zildjian, an old Turkish firm that keeps the exact blend of metals used a closely guarded secret.

*Zildjian*

### MUSIC FACTS

• European musical notation developed in A.D. 800-1100.

• The word *piano* comes from the Italian *piano e forte*, meaning "soft and loud."

• Making a classical guitar takes a lot of wood, about 85% of which is thrown away.

# Recording sound

In 1877, Thomas Edison invented the phonograph, a device that could both record and play back sounds. The sounds were stored as indentations on a piece of aluminum wrapped around a rotating drum. Mechanical recording continued until the 1920s, when electric systems first appeared.

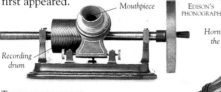

*Mouthpiece*

EDISON'S PHONOGRAPH

*Horn amplifies the sound.*

*Recording drum*

THE FIRST RECORDING
Edison's phonograph had a horn (not shown here) attached to the mouthpiece. A needle resting on the drum converted the indentations back into sounds, which were replayed through the horn.

*Needle rests in groove and vibrates as the disk revolves.*

EARLY GRAMOPHONE

*Flat disk sits on turntable.*

GRAMOPHONE
The first flat disk record player, or gramophone, was made by Emile Berliner in 1888. The playback mechanism was similar to that of Edison's phonograph, except that the sounds were stored on a flat disk rather than on a cylindrical drum.

TAPE RECORDER (1950s)

*Spools of magnetic tape*

*Loudspeaker*

## GETTING IT TAPED

Sound was first recorded onto magnetic tape in the 1920s. As the sound is recorded, tiny metal particles on the tape become magnetized. On replay, the particles produce electrical signals, which are reproduced as sound through the loudspeaker.

SONY WALKMAN

## PERSONAL STEREO

The Walkman was invented in 1979 by engineers at the Sony Corporation in Japan. Some thought that the Walkman's inability to record would make it difficult to sell, but it was an instant success.

*Cassette player*

*Earphones*

*Sound is stored as microscopic pits.*

COMPACT DISC

## COMPACT DISC

Launched in 1982, the compact disc (CD) stores sound digitally as a series of numbers. When it is replayed, the disc is scanned by a laser beam, which reads the encoded sound and allows it to be reproduced clearly.

### RECORDING FACTS

• Recorded music first went on sale in 1886.

• Modern magnetic tape came about as a result of scientists trying to improve sticky tape.

• Long-playing vinyl records (LPs) appeared in 1948 and played for five times longer than previous records.

# Radio

The invention of the radio transformed the entertainment business and led to a new information age. Radio was developed by Italian scientist Guglielmo Marconi, who started experimenting with radio waves in his parents' attic. In 1894, Marconi succeeded in sending radio waves across a room. By 1901, he was sending radio messages across the Atlantic.

**CRYSTAL SET**
In the 1920s, people used crystal sets to tune in to radio broadcasts. Inside the receiver was a carborundum (silicon compound) crystal and a fine wire, or "cat's whisker." By twiddling the wire, the listener could pick up the sound signals.

RADIO SET (1925)

Aerial

Volume control

Tuning knob

Headphones reproduce sound.

Crystal and cat's whisker

Wire carries signals to headphones.

**WIRELESS**
By the 1930s, crystal sets had been replaced by wirelesses with valves, which amplified the incoming signals. Some sets, like the one shown here, had aerials that could be rotated for the best reception. Later sets could be powered from wall sockets, which saved on batteries.

TRANSISTOR RADIO
In the 1950s, radio valves were replaced by transistors, which were smaller and used less power. The first transistor radio was built in 1954.

Tuning dial / Volume control

RADIO FACTS

• The world's first major radio station was set up in Pittsburgh, Pennsylvania, in 1920.

• Some experimental broadcasts consisted of an announcer reading a railway timetable.

• FM (Frequency Modulation) was invented in 1933.

Microphone cover

RADIO MICROPHONE
The ribbon microphone was used widely for broadcasting from the 1930s until the 1970s. A metallic ribbon inside the cover picked up the sound waves and converted them into electrical signals.

LOUDSPEAKERS
Early loudspeakers had horns, and groups of people would gather around them to listen to the radio. The modern type, which can fill a room with sound, was devised by Kellog and Rice in 1925.

LOUDSPEAKER

Cardboard cone

Magnetic field causes cone to vibrate.

RIBBON MICROPHONE WITH COVER

Case housing permanent magnet and coil

# Photography and film

In 1835, English scientist William Fox Talbot developed a photographic process, the principle of which is still used today. By coating paper with a silver compound, which darkens when exposed to light, he produced a negative image from which positives could be printed. By the 1900s, moving images could be recorded, and the film age began.

CAMERA OBSCURA (EARLY 1800S)

Lens

Curtain keeps out the light.

## CAMERA OBSCURA

The camera obscura had all the makings of a camera, but couldn't record images. As light shone through a small hole or a lens, an image was projected onto a flat surface inside the box.

Plate holder

Plate coated with light-sensitive chemicals

Rear section slides in and out to alter size of image.

## PLATE CAMERA

Photographic cameras that recorded images on plates, or glass sheets, were introduced in 1851. The plate was exposed for up to 30 seconds to capture a negative image.

BOXES OF ROLL FILM

Roll film was essential for later movie cameras

## ROLL FILM

In 1885, George Eastman devised rolls of plastic film to replace bulky photographic plates. Eastman also introduced a roll-film camera, which was both cheap and easy to use.

Lens tube

Fine-focusing control

Lens cover

PLATE CAMERA (1850S)

SLR CAMERA (1937)
Viewfinder
Film winder
Lens

A CLEARER PICTURE
A single-lens reflex (SLR) camera allows the photographer to see the exact image that will be recorded. A mirror and a prism inside the camera reflect the light from the lens to the viewfinder.

ON THE MOVE
Moving pictures are created by taking a series of still images in quick succession. The first successful movie camera was made in 1895 by the Lumière brothers of France.

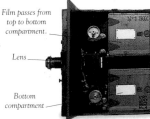

Film passes from top to bottom compartment.
Lens
Bottom compartment

MOVIE CAMERA (1909)

FILMING IN COLOR
This Technicolor camera recorded incoming light on separate films that were sensitive to red, blue, and green light. The films were then combined to make a full-color print that was projected onto a screen.

TECHNICOLOR CAMERA (1932)
Film spools
Lens

# Television and video

John Logie Baird first demonstrated television in 1926 at a famous department store in London, England. By 1934, more than 10,000 of his "televisors" had been sold. But the arrival of all-electronic television, which used cathode ray tubes, soon made the televisor obsolete and led to the first high-definition television broadcast.

*Speed control*

*Synchronizing control*

TELEVISOR (1926)

*Screen*

TELEVISOR
Baird's televisor worked on a system of spinning disks, which had been devised in 1884 by German scientist Paul Nipkow. The disks scanned the moving image and converted it into a series of electrical impulses, producing a poor-quality image on a tiny screen.

ELECTRONIC TELEVISION
By the late 1930s, all televisions used cathode ray tubes. The tubes projected electrons onto the screen, producing images of much higher quality than Baird's mechanical device could ever have done.

*Tuning control*

*Volume control*

TELEVISION (1950s)

### TELEVISION CAMERA

In 1924, Vladimir Zworykin devised a camera tube that could turn images into electrical signals so that they could be sent down a cable. Electronic cameras came into use in the 1930s.

### WATCHING IN COLOR

Inside a color television, three cathode ray tubes are combined into one. Each one shows pictures in either red, green, or blue, and the mixture of these colors on screen gives a full-color picture.

TELEVISION CAMERA (1936)

COLOR TELEVISION TUBE

*Three electron guns*

*Scanning coil sweeps electron beams across screen.*

Screen

### VIDEO RECORDER

A home video recorder receives signals from a television station and stores them on magnetic tape. When replayed, the magnetic patterns on the tape are turned into pictures.

*Drum carrying record/playback heads*

*Cassette*

VIDEO RECORDER (1970s)

---

### TELEVISION FACTS

• In 1936, a television set cost nearly as much as a small car.

• Color television was first broadcast successfully in 1953.

• Built in 1956, the first video recorder was the size of a piano and recorded onto tape that was 2 in (5 cm) wide.

# GAMES AND TOYS

PEOPLE HAVE ALWAYS entertained themselves with games or toys of some kind. Some of the games played today can be traced back to ancient times, while others are more recent inventions. Many games look incredibly simple, but the basic rules are often the product of an inventive mind.

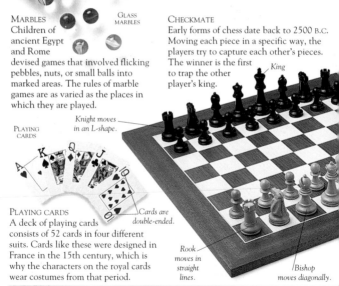

### MARBLES

GLASS MARBLES

Children of ancient Egypt and Rome devised games that involved flicking pebbles, nuts, or small balls into marked areas. The rules of marble games are as varied as the places in which they are played.

PLAYING CARDS

Knight moves in an L-shape.

Cards are double-ended.

### PLAYING CARDS

A deck of playing cards consists of 52 cards in four different suits. Cards like these were designed in France in the 15th century, which is why the characters on the royal cards wear costumes from that period.

### CHECKMATE

Early forms of chess date back to 2500 B.C. Moving each piece in a specific way, the players try to capture each other's pieces. The winner is the first to trap the other player's king.

King

Rook moves in straight lines.

Bishop moves diagonally.

## GAME AND TOY FACTS

- The first patented toy was a mechanical horse designed to teach people how to ride.

- Modern playing cards are based on Tarot cards, which were used for fortune-telling.

- Chess is derived from *chaturanga*, a Hindu dice game.

## DOMINOES

The game of dominoes originated in China and spread to Europe via Italian silk and spice traders. It is now played throughout the world.

*Adjacent numbers match.*

*The game starts with a high double.*

*Rubik's cube is made up of 27 smaller cubes.*

### RUBIK'S CUBE

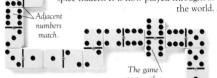

RUBIK'S CUBE

*A chessboard has 32 dark squares and 32 light squares.*

In 1980, Hungarian professor Ernö Rubik introduced a simple but infuriating puzzle that was to make him a multimillionaire. The object of the puzzle is to arrange the cube as it is shown here, so that each face is a uniform color.

GAME BOY

*Visual display*

*Each face of the cube can pivot around the center.*

### GAME BOY

Since the 1970s, electronic games have become increasingly popular. In 1989, the Nintendo company of Japan launched the Game Boy, a handheld video game player that proved popular with children of all ages.

*Control button*

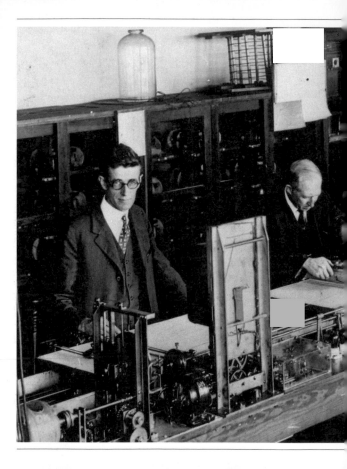

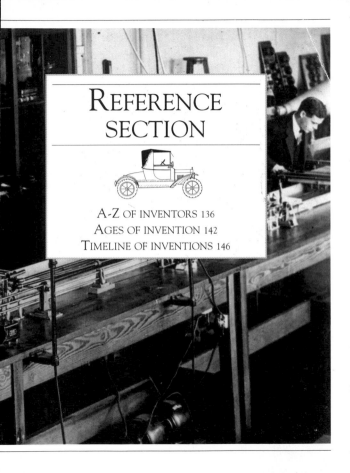

# REFERENCE SECTION

# A-Z OF INVENTORS

THE STORY OF INVENTION is one of human ingenuity and imagination. Many of the people who were inspired to invent objects that changed our world are as fascinating to read about as their creations. Here is a selection of some of the most interesting inventors.

ARCHIMEDES

Greek mathematician and inventor Archimedes (c.287-212 B.C.) is famous for leaping from his bath with a loud cry of "Eureka!" because he had figured out how and why things floated. He invented the siege engine, which the ancient Greeks used in battle, and he gave his name to a screw pump used for raising water. He also founded the science of hydrostatics – the study of the forces exerted by fluids.

ARCHIMEDES' SCREW

BELL, ALEXANDER GRAHAM

Alexander Graham Bell (1847-1922) was born in Scotland and emigrated to Canada in 1870. A teacher of the deaf, Bell was interested in trying to convert speech into electrical signals that could be sent down a wire. He patented the first working telephone in 1876, and a year later he traveled to England to promote his invention. Bell joined forces with American inventor Thomas Edison, and together they built several new telephones.

DA VINCI, LEONARDO

Italian artist Leonardo da Vinci (1452-1519) produced drawings of many complex machines, some of which suggested ways of traveling at speed, or even flying. Unfortunately, it was not possible to construct any of these machines in an age when there were neither the materials nor the technical know-how to build them.

RECONSTRUCTION OF ONE OF DA VINCI'S FLYING MACHINES

## DAIMLER, GOTTLIEB

DAIMLER'S MOTORCYCLE (1882)

Gottlieb Daimler (1834-1900) built the first roadworthy motor cycle in 1885. In 1926, he joined forces with fellow German Karl Benz, and together they formed the successful Daimler-Benz motor company. Daimler also worked closely with engineer Nikolaus Otto to develop a lightweight, high-speed engine that could run on gasoline. He first tried out his engine on a wooden-framed motorcycle (shown here).

## EDISON, THOMAS

American Thomas Edison (1847-1931) was expelled from school because his teachers thought he was a slow learner. Despite this, he became one of the world's greatest inventors. In 1871, Edison devised a ticker-tape machine, which brought financial news instantly to stock exchanges. The profits from this invention enabled him to set up a research laboratory and turn invention into an industry. His later inventions included the electric light bulb and the gramophone.

## FARADAY, MICHAEL

ROTATION APPARATUS (1821)

The son of a blacksmith, British scientist Michael Faraday (1791-1867) was apprenticed to a bookbinder. The books that he worked with sparked off a lifelong interest in science, and in 1813 he started work as an assistant at the Royal Institution in London, England. Although he was not strictly an inventor, Faraday discovered various electrical principles that were used in other inventions, such as the telephone and the electric motor.

## GALILEI, GALILEO

At a time when European scientists still clung to ancient Greek ideas, Italian Galileo Galilei (1564-1642) challenged many people's beliefs. Galileo was a mathematician, an astronomer, and a philosopher who came up with many ingenious inventions, from a primitive thermometer to an improved telescope. He also discovered that the swing of a pendulum could be used to regulate a clock and that the Earth moves around the Sun.

### GUTENBERG, JOHANNES

German-born Johannes Gutenberg (1400-1468) is regarded as the inventor of printing. Although the Chinese had invented ways of printing hundreds of years earlier, Gutenberg brought several techniques together, making the printing process much less laborious. His most ingenious invention was the idea of casting individual letters that could be assembled quickly into a block of type and fitted into a printing press.

### HOOKE, ROBERT

Robert Hooke (1635-1703) was a British scientist and architect who was asked to oversee the rebuilding of London after the Great Fire in 1666. During his lifetime, Hooke came up with several important inventions, including a balance spring for regulating watches, various instruments for navigation, and an improved microscope that enabled him to carry out important biological studies.

HOOKE'S MICROSCOPE (1660s)

### HUYGENS, CHRISTIAAN

The son of a Dutch poet, Christiaan Huygens (1629-1693) developed Galileo's ideas of the effect of gravity and the motions of the planets. He was interested in lenses and telescopes and suggested that light travels in waves. He was the first to see Saturn's rings, and he also discovered Saturn's fourth moon. Huygens used Galileo's discovery of the regular swing of a pendulum to build the first pendulum clock.

### KAY, JOHN

John Kay (1704-c.1780) was born in England and educated in France. He invented the flying shuttle, which was eagerly adopted by textile manufacturers who wanted to increase their output but who refused to give Kay any money for his idea. In 1753, Kay's house was attacked by angry textile workers who had lost their jobs as a result of his invention. Kay fled to France, where he died in poverty.

HAND LOOM

## KNIGHT, MARGARET

American inventor Margaret Knight (1839-1914) designed a machine for making the square-based paper bags that are often used for carrying groceries. Knight's invention brought her a great deal of public attention, since social convention in the 19th century meant that there were very few female inventors. Her local newspaper described her as a "woman Edison."

KNIGHT'S PAPER BAG MACHINE (1879)

## LIPPERSHEY, HANS

Dutch eyeglass-maker Hans Lippershey (c.1570-1619) realized that lenses could do more than just correct his clients' eyesight. He used convex

(outward-curving) lenses to correct long sight and concave (inward-curving) lenses to correct short sight. When he looked through both lenses together, Lippershey found that distant objects appeared closer. This discovery led to the invention of the telescope, which he patented in 1608.

## LISTER, JOSEPH

British surgeon Joseph Lister (1827-1912) was greatly influenced by his father (also called Joseph), who designed a microscope that he used to examine blood cells and body tissues. Continuing the family tradition, Lister made important discoveries about blood-clotting and the inflammation of blood vessels. He also introduced antiseptics, which dramatically reduced the incidence of death during surgery.

ANTISEPTIC SPRAY (1875)

## MAIMAN, THEODORE

American physicist Theodore Maiman (b.1927) gained a PhD in 1955 and started work on a maser, a device that was used to detect radio waves from

space. Maiman came up with the idea of using the same principle to produce light, and in 1960 he built the first working laser. The laser light was more intense than anything that had been seen before, and it now has all kinds of uses, from bar code readers to delicate surgery.

### MARCONI, MARCHESE GUGLIELMO

Guglielmo Marconi (1874-1937) had an Irish mother and
an Italian father. In 1894 he began experimenting
with radio waves, which had been discovered six
years earlier by German scientist Heinrich Hertz.
Marconi invented an aerial that increased the range of
transmission, and he soon realized that "wireless" messages
could reach almost anywhere. In 1901, he sent the
first radio message from Europe across the Atlantic.

RADIO
AERIAL

### MONTGOLFIER, JOSEPH AND JACQUES

French brothers
Joseph (1740-1810)
and Jacques (1745-
1799) Montgolfier
were the sons
of a paper-bag
manufacturer.
After noticing

that paper bags filled with hot air
could float upward, they set about
building the world's first hot-air
balloon. Made from reinforced
flameproof paper, and filled
with hot air from a fire below,
the balloon made its first
successful flight in 1783.

### MORSE, SAMUEL

American portrait painter Samuel Morse (1791-
1872) was interested in using electricity and
magnetism to send messages over long distances.
Working at the same time as telegraph inventors
Charles Wheatstone and William Cooke, Morse
devised his famous dot-dash code, which is still
used today. The code saves time because the
most common letters have the shortest codes.

MORSE CODE
MACHINE

### SHOCKLEY, WILLIAM

Together with John
Bardeen and William
Brattain, William
Shockley (1910-1989)
made the first working
transistor on Christmas
Eve, 1947. For years,
Shockley's team had

searched for a replacement for valves,
which were used in early televisions,
radios, and computers. Valves were
bulky and unreliable, and they gave
off a lot of heat. Transistors began
to replace valves by 1960 and led to
the complex yet tiny "chips," which
are universal in modern electronics.

## WATT, JAMES

James Watt (1736-1819) was a Scotsman who made scientific instruments for a living. In 1763, after studying the pumping action of Newcomen's steam engine, Watt made some improvements that enabled the engine to drive wheels, paddles, and propellers. These improvements, which involved turning the up-and-down motion of the piston into rotation, had a huge impact on Europe's Industrial Revolution.

## WHITTLE, FRANK

Frank Whittle (b.1907) joined the Royal Air Force in 1923 and patented the jet engine seven years later. The engine was built for high-speed, high-altitude flight, and was to replace the piston engine, which could not work in the cold, thin air at high altitudes. However, the first jet engines were not built until the late 1930s, when the metals needed to withstand the high temperatures in the new engine became available.

WHITTLE'S JET ENGINE (c.1940)

## WRIGHT, ORVILLE AND WILBUR

American brothers Orville (1871-1948) and Wilbur (1867-1912) Wright were self-taught aeronauts. In 1903, they built and flew the world's first successful powered airplane. Because they were bicycle-makers by trade, the brothers knew how to make machines both light and strong. By 1905, their *Flyer III* could turn and bank, fly in circles, and perform figures-of-eight.

## ZWORYKIN, VLADIMIR

Vladimir Zworykin (1889-1982) studied physics in Leningrad and emigrated to the US in 1919. Zworykin was obsessed with television, and in 1923 he devised the iconoscope, an essential component of the electronic television camera. Six years later, he started to work for the Radio Corporation of America, who believed that television would become big business. Despite America's head start, Britain's television service was the first on the air in 1936.

WHEEL

# AGES OF INVENTION

WHEN AND WHERE did inventions originate? From ancient times until recent years, many inventions can be linked to specific times and places. The ancient civilizations of Mesopotamia, Egypt, Greece, and Rome were all important centers of invention, while more recent innovations from Europe, North America, and the Pacific Rim have been important for economic and industrial growth.

## Invention in the ancient world

By about 500 B.C., many fundamental inventions and discoveries had already been made. Metalworking, building, surveying, and measuring were all developed in their basic forms by the end of the first millenium B.C. This period also saw the birth of science, as philosophers craved a greater knowledge and understanding of how things worked.

EARLY POTTERS

MESOPOTAMIA About 5,500 years ago, at the start of the Bronze Age, several cities were emerging in the region between the Euphrates and Tigris rivers – an area later known as Mesopotamia. The people who lived in this "cradle of civilization" came up with many great inventions, including the wheel, which was used for pottery and transportation.

ANCIENT EGYPT
Egypt was reaching the peak of its power

PYRAMID

and achievement by about 1500 B.C. Around this time, the Egyptians devised ways of moving huge stones, which enabled them to construct pyramids, temples, and other impressive structures. They were also pioneers in boat-building, sailing, and the use of early medical treatments.

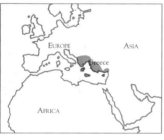

ANCIENT GREECE
From around the 6th century B.C., the Mediterranean region was ruled by

THE PARTHENON

the Greeks. The Greeks were accomplished architects and keen travelers, navigators, and seafarers. Greek philosophers introduced new ways of thinking, which influenced technology and laid the foundations of modern science.

ANCIENT ROME
By A.D. 100, the Roman Empire had spread from northern Europe to

ROAD-BUILDING

north Africa and the eastern Mediterranean. Such conquests demanded invention for war machines, transportation, and communication. The invention of concrete enabled the Romans to build a huge network of roads, some of which are still used today.

# Invention in the modern world

Many inventions that are used today had their origins in China. Some of these inventions remained unknown to the rest of the world for many years. However, the development of trading links in the 14th century meant that some of these inventions were taken to Europe by traveling merchants. At the close of the 20th century, Japan, Taiwan, and other countries of the Pacific Rim have become important centers of invention and innovation and are now enjoying the world's fastest economic growth.

PRINTING

## CHINA

From about 1000 B.C. to about A.D. 1000, a stream of ideas and inventions were emerging in China. In particular, the rule of the T'ang emperors (A.D. 618-906) was a time of great innovation. Among other things, the Chinese invented paper, printing, gunpowder, the magnetic compass, and a fine porcelain, which is still called "china."

NAVIGATING INSTRUMENTS

## RENAISSANCE

In the 14th and 15th centuries, a renaissance (or rebirth) of interest in Greek and Roman art, architecture, and literature swept across Europe. This period also saw the growth of modern science and the arrival of many new inventions, which were taken to Europe by Greek scholars fleeing from their Turkish enemies.

STEAM
LOCOMOTIVE

INDUSTRIAL REVOLUTION
The Industrial Revolution began in England and spread rapidly through Europe during the 18th century. It was a period of great innovation, triggered off by the use of water and then steam power to extract natural resources and to provide the energy and power needed for industry and transportation.

SKYSCRAPER

UNITED STATES OF AMERICA
In the 19th century, the US emerged as a powerful industrial nation. A rapidly growing population and a continent with seemingly unlimited natural resources provided the key to this growth. During this time, the US advanced in many areas of industry, including communication, engineering, transportation, and entertainment.

BULLET TRAIN

PACIFIC RIM
For centuries, differences in religion and culture kept the East and the West divided. Japan was the first country to rise above this, and by the 1970s Japanese companies were producing cars, motorcycles, and electronic goods that sold all over the world. Today, the success of industry in the Pacific Rim is overtaking that of the West.

# TIMELINE OF INVENTIONS

EXAMPLES OF HUMAN INVENTION and discovery can be traced back hundreds of thousands of years. The charts on the following pages list some key inventions and show how invention has progressed from early times to the present day.

| 20,000 B.C. | | | A.D. 1 |
|---|---|---|---|
| | 15,000 B.C. | 10,000 B.C. | 5000 B.C. |
| **INVENTIONS** • BONE NEEDLES (c.20,000 B.C.) • PAINTBRUSH (c.18,000 B.C.) • MAMMOTH-BONE HUTS (c.18,000 B.C.) | • HARPOONS (c.13,000 B.C.) • BASKET WEAVING (c.12,000 B.C.) • POTTERY VESSELS (c.10,500 B.C.) | • FISHING NETS (c.10,000 B.C.) • GRINDSTONES (c.10,000 B.C.) • COMB (c.8000 B.C.) • DUGOUT BOATS (c.7500 B.C.) • SPINDLE (c.7000 B.C.) • COPPER SMELTING (c.6500 B.C.) • BRICKS (c.6000 B.C.) • WHEELS (c.5500 B.C.) | • SAILING VESSELS (4000-3000 B.C.) • PLOW (c.3500 B.C.) • CUNEIFORM SCRIPT (4000-3000 B.C.) • ABACUS (c.3000 B.C.) • BARBED FISHHOOKS (c.3000 B.C.) • HORSERIDING (c.2000 B.C.) • IRON SMELTING (2000-1500 B.C.) • CALENDAR (1747 B.C.) • COINS (c.600 B.C.) |
| **WORLD EVENTS** • c.20,000 B.C. Stone tools are developed. • c.18,000 B.C. The last ice age reaches its coldest phase. | • 13,500-10,000 B.C. The last ice age comes to an end. • c.11,000 B.C. Dogs are domesticated. | • c.10,000 B.C. Woolly mammoths become extinct. • 9000-8000 B.C. Crop farming begins in the Middle East. | • c.3500 B.C. The Bronze Age begins. • c.2400 B.C. The first city-states are established in Mesopotamia. |

| A.D. 1 | | | A.D. 1500 |
|---|---|---|---|
| | | A.D. 500 | A.D. 1000 |
| **EVERYDAY LIFE** | • DOMED ROOF (c.A.D. 124) | | • SPECTACLES (A.D. 1268)<br>• MECHANICAL CLOCK (A.D. 1280) |
| **TRADE AND INDUSTRY** | • HORSESHOES (c.A.D. 50)<br>• WHEELBARROW (A.D. 200-300) | • WINDMILL (A.D. 650)<br>• PAPER MONEY (A.D. 800-900)<br>• WHEELED PLOW (A.D. 950) | • LACEMAKING (A.D. 1300-1350)<br>• STANDARD YARD (A.D. 1305)<br>• OIL PAINTS (A.D. 1400) |
| **SCIENCE AND COMMUNICATION** | • PAPER (A.D. 105) | • BOOK-PRINTING (A.D. 868)<br>• GUNPOWDER (A.D. 800-900) | • LENSES (c.A.D. 1000)<br>• CAMERA OBSCURA (c.A.D. 1000)<br>• PRINTING PRESS (A.D. 1450) |
| **TRAVEL AND EXPLORATION** | • STIRRUPS (A.D. 350)<br>• ASTROLABE (A.D. 400-500) | | • PADDED HORSE COLLAR (A.D. 900-1000)<br>• MAGNETIC COMPASS (A.D. 1100)<br>• STERNPOST RUDDER (c.A.D. 1200) |
| **ENTERTAINMENT AND LEISURE** | | | • MUSICAL NOTATION (A.D. 800-1100) |
| **WORLD EVENTS** | • A.D. 100 The Romans set up trade links with southern India and Sri Lanka.<br>• A.D. 300 Christianity becomes the official religion of the Roman Empire. | • A.D. 600 Islam spreads through the Middle East and northern Africa.<br>• A.D. 618 The T'ang dynasty rises to power in China. | • A.D. 1271 Italian explorer Marco Polo leaves Venice for China.<br>• A.D. 1346 Bubonic plague sweeps through Europe and Asia. |

| 1500 | | | 1699 |
|---|---|---|---|
| | 1550 | 1600 | 1650 |
| **EVERYDAY LIFE** | • WATCH (c.1500) | • FLUSHING TOILET (1596) | | • PENDULUM CLOCK (1657) <br> • SPIRIT LEVEL (1661) |
| **TRADE AND INDUSTRY** | | • KNITTING MACHINE (1589) | | |
| **SCIENCE AND COMMUNICATION** | | • PENCIL (1565) <br> • COMPOUND MICROSCOPE (1590) | • REFRACTING TELESCOPE (1608) <br> • PASCAL'S CALCULATOR (1642) | • IMPROVED MICROSCOPE (1665) <br> • REFLECTING TELESCOPE (1668) |
| **TRAVEL AND EXPLORATION** | | • MERCATOR PROJECTION MAP (1569) | • STAGECOACH (c.1620) <br> • SUBMARINE (1624) | |
| **ENTERTAINMENT AND LEISURE** | | | | |
| **WORLD EVENTS** | • 1526 The powerful Mogul empire is founded in India. <br> • c.1530 The trans-Atlantic slave trade is established. | • 1540 The Ottoman empire in Asia reaches its peak. <br> • 1577 Francis Drake sets sail on his round-the-world voyage. | • 1620 Pilgrims land in America aboard the *Mayflower*. <br> • 1644 The Manchu dynasty is founded in China. | • 1680s The Ashanti kingdom of West Africa is established. <br> • 1682 Halley spots the comet that's now named after him. |

| 1700 | | | 1899 |
|---|---|---|---|
| | 1750 | 1800 | 1850 |
| **EVERYDAY LIFE** | • FRANKLIN STOVE (1740) | • OIL LAMP WITH HOLLOW WICK (1784)<br>• VACCINE (1796) | • MATCHES (1827)<br>• LAWN MOWER (1830) | • ELECTRIC LIGHT BULB (c.1880)<br>• COMPACT ELECTRIC MOTOR (1899) |
| **TRADE AND INDUSTRY** | • NEWCOMEN'S STEAM ENGINE (1712)<br>• FLYING SHUTTLE (1733) | • WATT'S STEAM ENGINE (1782)<br>• COTTON GIN (1792) | • JACQUARD LOOM (1805)<br>• REAPING MACHINE (1834) | • POWERED WOOL CLIPPERS (1860s)<br>• STEAM TURBINE GENERATOR (1884) |
| **SCIENCE AND COMMUNICATION** | • MERCURY THERMOMETER (1714)<br>• CENTIGRADE SCALE (1742) | • LIGHTNING ROD (1752)<br>• SPRING BALANCE (1776)<br>• METRIC SYSTEM (1795) | • BATTERY (1800)<br>• POSTAGE STAMPS (1840)<br>• ANESTHETICS (1846) | • TYPEWRITER (1870)<br>• TELEPHONE (1876)<br>• RADIO (1894) |
| **TRAVEL AND EXPLORATION** | • OCTANT (1731) | • SEXTANT (1757)<br>• HOT-AIR BALLOON (1783)<br>• PROPELLER (1790s) | • STEAM LOCOMOTIVE (1803)<br>• PEDAL BICYCLE (1839)<br>• IRON SHIPS (1840) | • MOTOR CAR (1885)<br>• SAFETY BICYCLE (1885)<br>• DIESEL ENGINE (1892) |
| **ENTERTAINMENT AND LEISURE** | • PIANO (1709) | | • SAXOPHONE (1846) | • PLATE CAMERA (1851)<br>• PHONOGRAPH (1877)<br>• GRAMOPHONE (1888) |
| **WORLD EVENTS** | • 1724 The Russian Academy of Sciences is founded.<br>• 1737 Earthquake kills 300,000 people in India. | • 1750 The Chinese take over the state of Tibet.<br>• 1789 The Social Revolution begins in France. | • 1815 Napoleon is defeated at the Battle of Waterloo.<br>• 1839 The Opium War begins between Britain and China. | • 1845 The potato famine hits Ireland.<br>• 1854 Russia is defeated in the Crimean War. |

## 1900                                                    1949

| | 1900 | 1910 | 1920 | 1930 | 1940 |
|---|---|---|---|---|---|
| **EVERYDAY LIFE** | • SAFETY RAZOR (1903)<br>• WASHING MACHINE (1907) | • DOMESTIC ELECTRIC REFRIGERATOR (1913)<br>• ZIPPER (1914) | • HAIR DRYER (1920)<br>• POP-UP TOASTER (1927) | • NYLON (1934)<br>• INSTANT COFFEE (1938) | • AEROSOL CAN (1941)<br>• MICROWAVE OVEN (1946) |
| **TRADE AND INDUSTRY** | | • STAINLESS STEEL (1913)<br>• ASSEMBLY LINE (1913) | • SYNTHETIC RUBBER (1927) | • POLYETHYLENE (1933)<br>• PHOTOCOPIER (1938) | • NUCLEAR REACTOR (1942) |
| **SCIENCE AND COMMUNICATION** | • ELECTRO-CARDIOGRAPH (1903)<br>• THERMIONIC VALVE (1906) | • NUCLEAR MODEL OF THE ATOM (1911) | • ANTIBIOTICS (1928) | • ELECTRON MICROSCOPE (c.1931)<br>• BALLPOINT PEN (1938) | • CIRCUIT BOARD (1943)<br>• COMPUTER (1946)<br>• TRANSISTOR (1947) |
| **TRAVEL AND EXPLORATION** | • DISK BRAKES (1902)<br>• WRIGHT FLYER (1903)<br>• CAR SEAT BELT (1903) | • ELECTRIC TRAFFIC LIGHTS (1914)<br>• WINDSHIELD WIPERS (1916) | • HIGHWAY (1921) | • JET ENGINE (1930)<br>• CAT'S EYES (1935)<br>• RADAR (1935) | • RADIAL-PLY TIRES (1949) |
| **ENTERTAINMENT AND LEISURE** | • MECCANO (1901)<br>• TEDDY BEAR (1903) | | • TELEVISOR (1926) | • ELECTRIC GUITAR (1932)<br>• STEREO RECORDING (1933) | • SCUBA (1942)<br>• LONG-PLAYING RECORD (1948) |
| **WORLD EVENTS** | • 1901 Marconi radios across the Atlantic.<br>• 1904 Work starts on the Panama Canal. | • 1914 World War I breaks out.<br>• 1915 Einstein develops theory of relativity. | • 1920 Gandhi starts movement against British rule in India.<br>• 1929 US Stock Exchange crashes. | • 1936 Civil war starts in Spain.<br>• 1939 World War II begins. | • 1945 Atom bomb destroys Hiroshima.<br>• 1948 Policy of apartheid begins in South Africa. |

| 1950 | | | | 1999 |
|---|---|---|---|---|
| | 1960 | 1970 | 1980 | 1990 |
| **EVERYDAY LIFE** <br>• STEAM IRON (c.1955) <br>• VELCRO (1956) <br>• LYCRA (1959) | • TEFLON COOKWARE (1960) <br>• FLYMO (1963) | • FOOD PROCESSOR (1971) <br>• DIGITAL WATCH (1971) | | • SELF-HEATING CANNED FOOD (1991) |
| **TRADE AND INDUSTRY** <br>• CREDIT CARD (1950) <br>• NUCLEAR POWER STATION (1954) | • INDUSTRIAL ROBOT (1962) | • BAR CODES (1974) | • SMART CARD (1982) | • NUCLEAR FUSION (1990s) |
| **SCIENCE AND COMMUNICATION** <br>• BIRTH CONTROL PILL (1954) <br>• SILICON CHIP (1959) | • COMMUNI-CATION SATELLITE (1962) <br>• WORD PROCESSOR (1964) | • X-RAY SCANNER (1972) <br>• PERSONAL COMPUTER (1978) | • POST-IT NOTES (1981) <br>• ARTIFICIAL HEART (1982) | • VIDEOPHONE (1991) <br>• VOICE RECOGNITION (1990s) |
| **TRAVEL AND EXPLORATION** <br>• SPACE SATELLITE (1957) <br>• HOVERCRAFT (1959) | • JUMBO JET (1969) | • CATALYTIC CONVERTER (1979) | • SPACE SHUTTLE (1981) | |
| **ENTERTAINMENT AND LEISURE** <br>• TRANSISTOR RADIO (1954) <br>• VIDEO RECORDER (1956) | • SKATEBOARD (1963) <br>• CASSETTE RECORDER (1963) | • HOME VIDEO GAMES (1972) <br>• WALKMAN (1979) | • RUBIK'S CUBE (1980) <br>• COMPACT DISC (1982) | • VIRTUAL REALITY (1990s) |
| **WORLD EVENTS** <br>• 1953 Scientists reveal DNA's structure. <br>• 1954 Hillary and Tenzing climb Everest. | • 1966 Cultural Revolution starts in China. <br>• 1969 US astronauts land on the Moon. | • 1973 Australia's Sydney Opera House is built. <br>• 1978 The first test-tube baby is born. | • 1986 Nuclear reactor explodes at Chernobyl. <br>• 1989 The Berlin Wall comes down. | • 1990 Iraq invades Kuwait. <br>• 1991 Slovenia and Croatia announce their independence. |

# Resources

## UNITED STATES

**Age of Steam Railroad Museum**
Fairground-State
Fair of Texas
Dallas, TX 75226

**Arts & Industries Building**
900 Jefferson, SW
Washington, DC 20560

**Boston Public Library & Eastern Massachusetts Regional Public Library System**
Copley Square
Boston, MA 02117

**Brooklyn Children's Museum**
145 Brooklyn Avenue
Brooklyn, NY 11213

**Brooklyn Public Library System**
Grand Army Plaza
Brooklyn, NY 11238

**Capital Children's Museum**
800 Third Street, NE
Washington, DC 20560

**Children's Hands-on Museum**
2213 University Blvd.
Tuscaloosa, AL 35403

**Children's Museum**
Museum Wharf
300 Congress Street
Boston, MA 02210

**Cornell University Libraries***
Ithaca, NY 14853

**Cumberland Science Museum**
800 Ridley Blvd.
Nashville, TN 37203

**The Exploratorium**
3601 Lyon Street
San Francisco, CA 94123

**The Farmers' Museum**
Lake Road
Cooperstown, NY 13326

**The Field Museum of Natural History**
Roosevelt Road at Lake Shore Drive
Chicago, IL 60605

**Franklin Institute Science Museum & Planetarium**
20th & Benjamin Franklin Hwy.
Philadelphia, PA 19103

**Free Library of Philadelphia**
Logan Square
Philadelphia, PA 19103

**Henry Ford Museum & Greenfield Village**
20900 Oakwood Blvd.
Dearborn, MI 48121

**Kidspace-A Participatory Museum**
390 South El Molino
Pasadena, CA 91101

**Los Angeles Public Library System**
433 S. Spring
Los Angeles, CA 90013

**Massachusetts Institute of Technology (MIT) Libraries***
Room 14S-216
Cambridge, MA 02139

**Museum of Fine Arts**
465 Huntington Avenue
Boston, MA 02115

**Museum of Television & Radio**
25 W. 52nd Street
New York, NY 10019

**Museum of Transportation**
3015 Barrett Station Rd.
St. Louis, MO 63122

**National Air & Space Museum**
Smithsonian Institution
Sixth Street &
Independence Ave., SW
Washington, DC 20560

**New York University Elmer Bobst Library***
70 Washington Square
South New York,
NY 10012

**Ohio State University Libraries William Oxley Thompson Memorial Library***
1858 Neil Avenue Mall
Columbus, OH 43210

**Please Touch Museum**
210 North 21st Street
Philadelphia, PA 19103

**Printers Row Printing Museum**
731 S. Plymouth Court
Chicago, IL 60648

**National Museum of American History**
Smithsonian Institution
Washington, DC 20560

**Stanford University Library***
Stanford, CA 94305

**State University of New York at Buffalo University Libraries***
432 Capen Hall
Buffalo, NY 14260

**University of Arizona Library***
Tucson, AZ 85721

**University of Florida Libraries***
210 Library West
Gainesville, FL 32611

**University of Minnesota Libraries Twin Cities 499 O. Meredith Wilson Library***
309 19th Avenue South
Minneapolis, MN 55455

**University of Utah Marriott Library***
Salt Lake City,
UT 84112

**University of Virginia Alderman Library***
Charlottesville,
VA 22903

CANADA

**McGill University Libraries***
3459 McTavish Street
Montreal, Quebec
H3A 1Y1

**University of Toronto Library System***
Toronto
Ontario
M5S 1A5

USEFUL ADDRESSES:

**Commissioner of Patents & Trademarks**
Washington, DC 20231

*It is advisable to call ahead to find out reader policies for college or university libraries.

# Index

# Index of inventors

# Acknowledgments

**Dorling Kindersley would like to thank:**
Heather Blackham, Kate Eagar, Myfanwy Hancock, and Carlton Hibbert for design assistance. Elise Bradbury, Deslie Lawrence, and Anderley Moore for editorial assistance. Caroline Potts and Robert Graham for picture research assistance. Hilary Bird for the index.

**Photographs by:**
Paul Bricknell, Martin Cameron, Peter Chadwick, Andy Crawford, Philip Dowell, Mike Dunning, Philip Gatwood, Steve Gorton, Ralph Hall, Peter Hayman, Chas Howson, Colin Keates, Gary Kevin, Dave King, Kevin Mallett, Ray Moller, Stephen Oliver, Daniel Pangbourne, Barry Richards, Tim Ridley, Dave Rudkin, Karl Shone, James Stevenson, Clive Streeter, Matthew Ward, Adrian Whicher, Jerry Young, Michel Zabé

**Illustrations by:**
Russell Barnet, Rick Blakely, Peter Bull, Kuo Kang Chen, Stephen Conlin, Luciano Corbella, Nick Hewetson, Ray Hutchins (Linden Artists), John Hutchinson, Stan Johnson, Helen Lee, Jason Lewis, Louise Morley, Sergio, Taurus Graphics, Eric Thomas, Richard Ward, Gerry Wood, John Woodcock

**Picture credits:**

t = top b = bottom c = centre l = left r = right

The publisher would like to thank the following for their permission to reproduce their photographs:

Barclaycard 49b; Barclays Bank 49br; Birmingham International Airport Photo Library 107b; Black & Decker 27r; Bridgeman Art Library/Royal Geographical Society 117tr; British Library 89t; British Museum 48c; J. Allen Cash Photolibrary 47tr; Bruce Coleman: John Worrall 22-23, Gene Ahrens 52r, R. P. Carr 64tl; Mary Evans Picture Library 21tl; Explorer 36bl, 66l, 138c, 139t, 140b, 141t, 141c; Robert Harding Picture Library: R. J. Winwood 61tr, Robert Cundy 66r, Philip Craven 90r; Hulton Deutsch Collection 55tl, 111tl, 121tl, 131tl, 134-5; Janome New Home 19br; Mansell Collection 40tr; Medical Slide Library: Dr. Ian Williams 85bl; Moscow Museum 115r; Museum of Archaeology and Anthropology 86cr; Museum of London 64tr; NASA 115l; National Maritime Museum 121bl; National Motor Museum 110b; Peter Newark's Historical Pictures 112r; Robert Opie 25br, 17tr; Pictor International 105tr; Pilkington Glass Museum 27l; Pitt Rivers Museum 46tl; Post Office Archives 91b; Range/Bettman/UPI 139b, 141b; Reader's Digest (Australia) Pty Ltd. 37tl; Ann Ronan at Image Select 14l, 136c, 137t, 137b, 138t, 138b, 139t, 140t; Royal Museum of Scotland 38tr; St. Bride Printing Library front cover bl, 89c; Science Museum/Society & Science Picture Library 37br; Science Photo Library: Paul Schambroom 73br; Smith & Nephew Richards Ltd. 71tr; Smithsonian Institute 15br, 17tl, 17cl, 17c, 18b, 41bl, 49r, 55r, 61cl, 65br, 66b, 94b, 109cr, 130tl, 139tr; Tony Stone Images: Andy Sack 60bl, 114bl; Syndication International 15tr; Elizabeth Whiting & Associates 29tl.

Special thanks are due to the Science Museum for their permission to reproduce many of the photographs that appear in this book.

Sony and Walkman are registered trademarks of the Sony Corporation, Japan.

Every effort has been made to trace the copyright holders, and we apologize in advance for any unintentional omissions. We would be pleased to insert the appropriate acknowledgment in any subsequent edition of this publication.